INTEGRATING TECHNICAL ANALYSIS FOR THE INVESTOR

BC Low

Chartered Market Technician

Technical Analysis Consultancy
SINGAPORE

PUBLISHER
Technical Analysis Consultancy
www.taconsultancy.biz
Singapore
First Published as ebook 2014
2016 Print Edition
ISBN 978-981-09-8467-0

Dedicated to Connie,

Shi Ping & Shi Min

Acknowledgements

My wife, Connie Lim for her support and encouragement for me in writing this book. I am also thankful to Connie for reviewing this book's content.

Ms Low Shi-Ping for editing the book, in making it more readable to the average reader.

Mr Lye Ming-Chye for his consistent help as webmaster and in all IT matters relating to Technical Analysis Consultancy including the publishing of this book.

Charts in this book are plotted with charting software, Metastock which I have had the privilege of using for many years.

CONTENTS

Chapter 7 Timing with Moving Average Convergence Divergence (MACD) 89

Chapter 8 Integrating Trend, Timing & Price 112

FOREWORD

Although technical analysis has fascinated and inspired me for close to thirty years, it is not as widely accepted in the investor community. While I can understand why that is so, it is my hope that this book will change some attitudes towards technical analysis by showing how it can help the investor in the important investment decisions. I hope that the ideas in this book will help investors get more out of their investor dollars.

Many books on technical analysis have been written with the professional trader in mind. These books often deal with complex topics which maybe beyond the interest of the average investor. Other books adopt an 'encyclopaedia' approach which maybe too much for the average investor whose needs are less.

I believe the average investor seeks to learn key aspects of technical analysis to satisfy three important needs – firstly to identify a market's trend, secondly to identify reliable timing signals to enter and exit a position; and thirdly, to identify the price levels to enter and exit a position This book is written with these needs in mind.

However, this book is not intended to provide a "Black Box" to for investors to plug into. It will show how several public domain technical analysis tools can be better interpreted and integrated to help the investor. It begins with the author's personal interpretations of technical indicators familiar to many, namely moving averages, Bollinger Bands, Fibonacci Ratios, Stochastics, Moving Average Convergence

Divergence, selected price patterns and candlestick patterns. The approach is not to provide an exhaustive discussion of these techniques, since there are many other titles already in print to focus on each of the techniques covered. Rather it is to emphasize aspects of these techniques which when integrated and used together, will help the investor to combine the knowledge of a market's trend with the timing and price levels to enter and exit a position.

The investor is not a trader. His concern is for the longer term and making returns from taking positions over the long run. Over the years, I have paid special attention to the issue of using technical analysis for the longer term. As such, I will share my original technique of Time Frames, developed in the 1990's.

This book shares with investors the tools of technical analysis that I have used in the past 20 plus years. It draws on materials that have been used to educate a generation of students who studied technical analysis with me as part of a fulltime course in a Singapore college.

To those who already have some understanding of technical analysis, this book can add focus on integration, as well as the use of technical analysis for long term investment. To investors just starting out, I hope it will provide a strong framework so that technical analysis can be used to make investing a more profitable and enriching experience. Overall, I do hope this book will make a real difference to investors.

CHAPTER 1 - INTRODUCTION

Technical analysis is for the Investor too!

Technical analysis is the art and science that uses charting tools to tell us a market's trend, the timing and price levels to enter and exit the market. My approach in technical analysis focuses on integrating these three aspects – trend, price and timing using a combination of the most effective tools in each area based on my observation and use of technical analysis. To me it is not enough to just know the various indicators individually, but integrating them to achieve better results.

Technical Analysis is about Probability

As in other methods of forecasting, technical analysis is about improving the probability of getting the market right. There is no certainty that a technical indicator will deliver sure-win results since markets do not conform completely to any fixed pattern for too long beyond rising and falling. But with so much progress made in technical analysis, the probability of getting it right can be higher. Investors should be able to depend on it than on gut feel or hearsay.

On the other hand, no matter how good technical tools become, one can never be certain of an indicator being correct all the time. In addition, there is the element of judgment in interpreting technical signals such that two persons using the exact same indicator at one time may hold opposing views! There is the element of subjectivity.

Technical vs Fundamental Analysis

Both technical and fundamental approaches use different types of information to arrive at a view. Technical analysis is based on signals from indicators which apply to price – closing price alone or high, low and closing prices of each trading period. The advantage of the technical approach is that when a technical indicator is applied to different markets, it produces similar signals. There is economy of effort in that once an investor knows how a particular indicator works, he can use it in practically all markets.

Fundamental analysis uses supply and demand information within a market, which may be peculiar to that market. A great deal of information and research is needed to secure the relevant and key market information to provide the view. And the effort has to be repeated for each market.

For them to be effective, both technical and fundamental analyses involve a lot of effort. But in my view, one should aspire to excel in one of the two approaches because when practised well, either one is capable of delivering results.

Where does technical analysis work best?

Technical analysis works best when the market is large and no one player or group of players has the means to influence its price for a considerable period of time. If a market is small and can be easily influenced, then technical analysis becomes less effective. This is true in all markets - currencies, commodities and stocks, indices, etc.

With the explosive growth in technical analysis tools in recent years due to application of IT, technical analysis has become complex and involves multiple indicators. This adds sophistication but can also lead users of technical analysis to experience difficulty in practising the art – the so-called "analysis paralysis".

Holy Grail versus a Tool Box

The typical investor tends to look for the Holy Grail in technical analysis. This tendency is reinforced by famous techniques that have made headlines in the past. In my opinion, it is more effective to adopt a "tool box" approach in technical analysis. Basically, an investor need's are in key areas – he needs to know a market's trend, entry/exit timing and entry/exit prices. What the investor needs is a collection of good indicators to meet each of these requirements. After all, it is difficult to even find ONE good trend indicator, let alone a Holy Grail in which trend, timing and price signals are provided by just one indicator!

What an investor should do is to build up a tool box consisting of a small number of reliable indicators in each area of trend, timing and price. This is an on-going process, and when we discover better tools we can add them to our tool box and drop off those tools that have proved to be less effective over time.

We do not want too many indicators or duplicating indicators that end up confusing us!

What I offer in this book are a number of effective tools that can form the core of your own technical toolbox if you do not already have one. The indicators covered here are tools which have a proved track record over many years. If you already have your own toolbox, it is hoped that the indicators in this book will add more value to it.

It should also be pointed out here that the approach in this book is not to focus on the mathematical aspects of technical tools, but their applications and role in investing. Those interested in the more mathematical aspects are advised to refer to the many other books already available, which cover those aspects in greater depth.

Integration is Key

I hold the view that technical analysis must help the investor to integrate the three notions of trend, timing and price. The investor is faced with the question of knowing a market's current trend, and bases on that the timing and price to enter and exit the market. These three areas are inextricably linked. So while it is good to describe the trend, timing and pricing tools separately, it is much clearer if the linkages between these different tools are dealt with as well in any book.

Chapter 8 "Integrating Trend, Timing & Price" is therefore devoted to linking the various indicators covered in the earlier chapters. In Chapter 8, readers will be shown how the signals from different tools can act together at one point to help the investor to arrive at a better decision.

Another technique in this book to integrate different technical tools is by linking signals from one indicator to another indicator (in subsequent chapters) which provide supporting signals. This is done through the "Other Indicators" section found in some of the chapters.

Technical Analysis is also for long-term investment

Among investors and even practitioners of technical analysis, there is a common perception that technical analysis is only good for short-term trading. This misunderstanding of technical analysis is long and deep. I have pioneered the Time Frame Principle since the 1990s which involves the use of long term charts to look at long-term trends. This approach defines trends clearly by the time frame of the charts – daily, weekly, monthly, and so on. By using these longer term charts, and also **integrating them**, it is now possible to consistently provide long-term views of markets. Chapter 9 deals with this important issue of using technical analysis for investing; it also explains link between the longer term trends to the shorter term trend. It is hoped that this book will build up the notion that technical analysis is for the investor as well.

CHAPTER 2 - FORECASTING TREND WITH PRICE ACTION

Basics that matter!

Trend definition is the first priority of any investor looking at any market. If the trend is up, then the issue will be whether it is a new uptrend, or a mature one. If the uptrend is just beginning, then it is the time to put on the positions. If the trend is mature, then it may be time to liquidate some positions. In other words, the decision to buy or sell depends greatly on the trend.

If, however, the market trend is down, you should short the market or if you cannot do that, you should postpone buying until the trend turns up again. Either way, the trend should determine your basic investment decision. Going against the trend is not advisable because we do not know where and how long that trend will last. Once you know the trend, you can use the appropriate timing and price indicators to time your entry and your exit.

This chapter will focus on using only price action to decide on a trend. This is the most basic technique, without using any technical indicator at all. We will look at an important trend indicator, 10 and 40 Exponential Moving Averages in Chapter

3. For price action, there are three approaches which an investor can use to help him decide on a trend – price <u>level</u>, selected <u>price patterns</u>, and selected <u>candlestick patterns</u>.

These three areas of price action provide important evidence to support the view of a market trend which is determined primarily by 10/40 Exponential Moving Averages. At the right place and the right time, the price level, price patterns and certain candlestick patterns reinforce the view of the trend from the 10/40 Exponential Moving Average (EMA). In other words, in my approach at determining trend, price level, price patterns and candlestick patterns are not the most important tools. But they are basic enough and do play a part, but because of inherent weaknesses of these three techniques, I feel they should be accorded only a supporting role, and not a primary one in determining a trend.

DEFINING TREND WITH PRICE LEVELS

Price level is the most basic technique for an investor determine a market's trend. While it is by no means the definitive method, it provides a quick view of a trend and can be used in all markets.

Uptrend is a series of <u>higher highs</u>, <u>higher lows</u> and <u>higher closes</u>.
Downtrend is a series of <u>lower highs</u>, <u>lower lows</u> and <u>lower closes</u>.
Congestion is a series of <u>similar highs</u> and <u>lows</u>.

With this method of defining trend, the issue is in deciding which are the points to use as reference highs and lows to decide on higher highs/low, lower highs/lows. It takes some judgment and practice, but over time one learns.

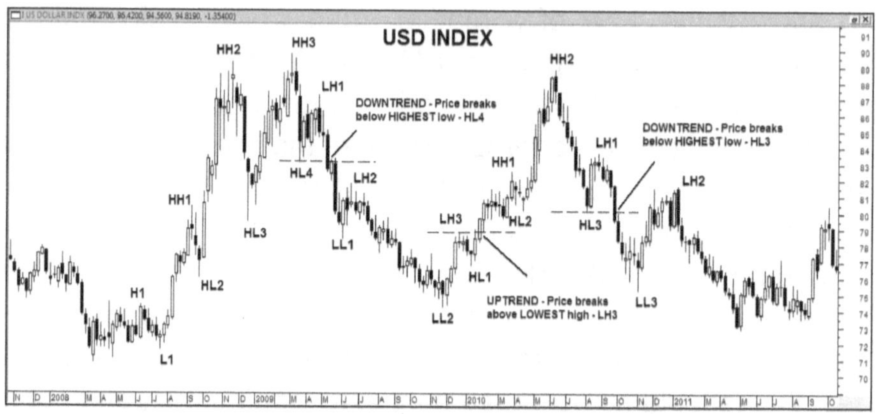

Chart 2.1: Market trend and change in trend as defined by highs and lows

An intermediate solution to decide on the trend is to monitor the bar-by-bar movement - if individual bars are progressively higher or lower, they do reinforce the existing trend.

Change in Trend

From Downtrend to Uptrend

A change begins when price breaks above the lowest high. A higher high subsequently forms, and if this is confirmed by a higher low, then the trend has changed by this method. (See Chart 2.1)

From Uptrend to Downtrend
This change begins when price breaks below the highest low. A lower low subsequently forms, and if this is confirmed by a lower high, then the trend has changed, going by this method. (See Chart 2.1)

The issue with this method is that waiting for the market to penetrate the previous highest low or lowest high to decide on a change in trend may mean giving away too much of the market to confirm a change in trend.

Also, the change to uptrend can be invalidated if the higher high and low are subsequently negated by a lower high and lower low, and vice versa. However such occurrences unless they are frequent, do not invalidate this simple yet usable method of defining trend.

Sideways or Congestion

This a situation when a market experiences similar highs and lows in a period of time. 'Similar' does not mean that highs and lows are exactly the same during the period, but the market is not exhibiting higher highs or lower lows.

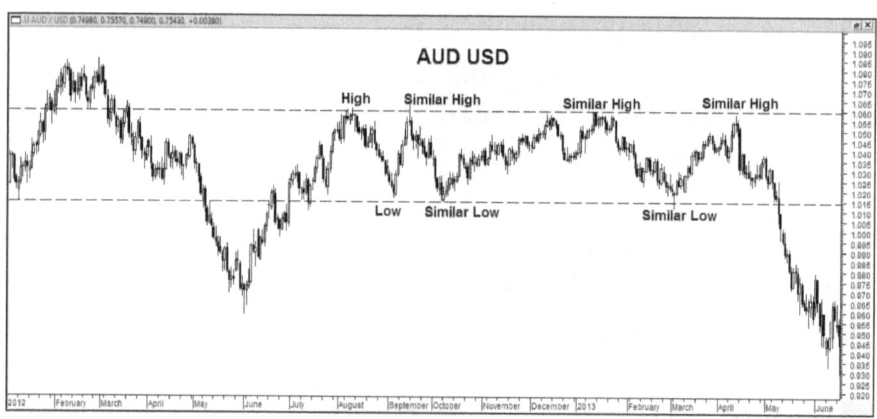

Chart 2.2: Congestion as defined by similar highs and lows

However, congestions are a temporary situation for a market. Eventually markets get back into a trend, up or down.

DEFINING TREND WITH SELECTED PRICE PATTERNS

Price patterns are among the oldest technical analysis tools in the books. They probably came into use as an intuitive approach from looking at price bars when no other technique was available. While I still find certain patterns valid in today's markets, I find that price patterns too subjective; one can argue inconclusively as to what is forming in the market at any one point in time. Also, some patterns are not commonly found, and failure in patterns does occur. So overall, I find price patterns may be overrated in defining a trend.

However, despite some reservations, I do believe that at the right place and the right time, some patterns are still useful. In particular, when they are integrated with powerful indicators such as 10/40 Exponential Moving Averages (Chapter 3), some price patterns can add significant value, and do reinforce the signals from the 10/40 Exponential Moving Averages (EMA).

In this chapter we will feature patterns that I have seen over the years and from various markets that are useful. The patterns are flag, breakaway gap, runaway gap, and the key reversal.

Flag

A Flag is a price pattern found in trending markets. It is a useful pattern to help the investor decide if the trend is in place. To some, when a flag is forming, it may look like a reversal. But if the investor is aware of Flags, then he will recognize that the trend will continue after the flag, and the Flag is just a correction.

A Flag is a **short-lived** phenomenon, from 2 bars up to 7 bars. Price moves against the current trend; if the trend is down, the Flag is a collection of rising bars, and vice versa. The price correction is **shallow**, and may stop at a short-term moving average line. Soon after the few bars in the Flag, the trend resumes in the original direction.

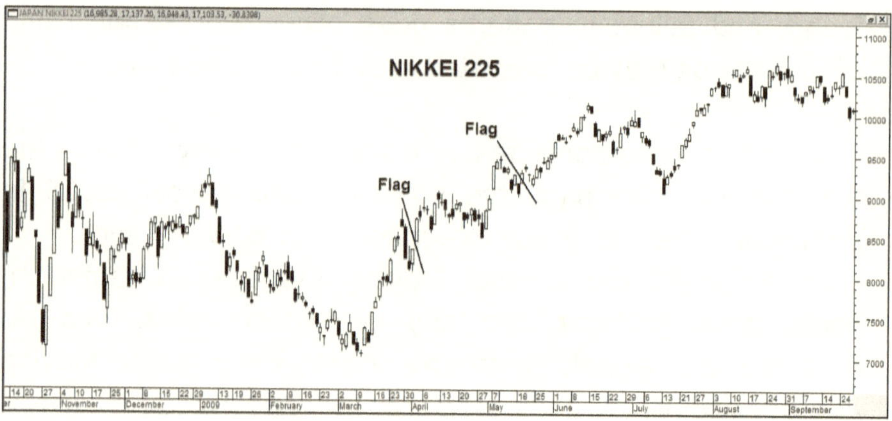

Chart 2.3: Flags in an uptrend

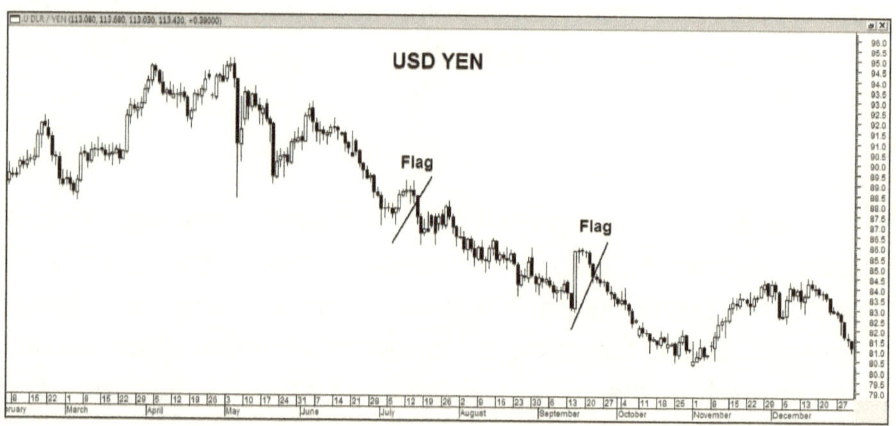

Chart 2.4: Flags in a downtrend

The important value of a Flag is also that it presents the investor with an opportunity to enter the market in a shallow correction. The exact entry level can be a moving average; as to which moving average, the issue will be covered in the Chapter 3 on 10/40 Exponential Moving Averages, and Chapter 8 on Integrating Trend, Price and Timing.

Other Indicators: Flags can be easily recognised when they occur as prices that trade OUTSIDE the Bollinger Bands (Chapter 4) for a few periods. As price trades back INTO the Bollinger Bands, the flag forms.

Gaps

Gaps are price areas which are not traded by a market between two price bars. There are 3 types of gaps - Common Gap, Breakaway Gap and Runaway Gap.

Common gaps are small and typically occur in congestions. They do not have much significance technically.

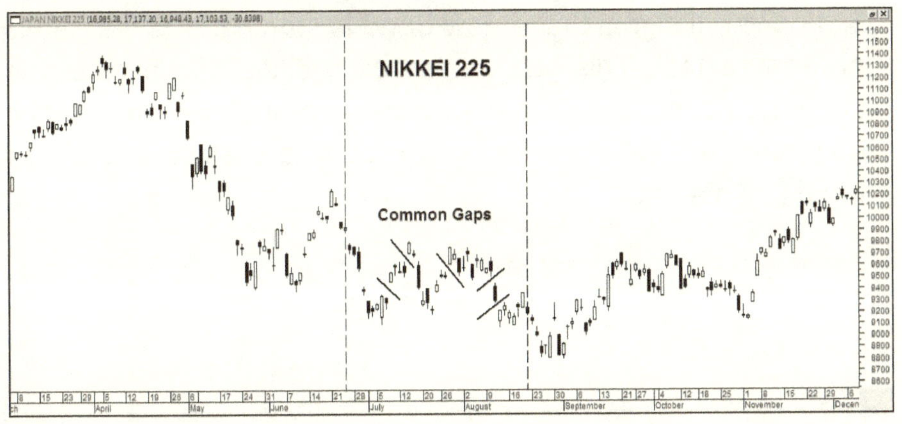

Chart 2.5: Common gaps

Breakaway Gap

In my view, this is one of the most important price patterns because the Breakaway Gap signals the start of a new trend, or the resumption of a trend which has paused. It typically is a reaction to important events which take place after a market has closed for the period, be it the day or week.

The Breakaway Gap can occur at a market top or bottom after a sizeable trend taken place. Reacting to important news, price suddenly trades dramatically away from the previous consolidation and creates a gap that runs opposite to the previous trend. A Breakaway Gap is typically sizeable, and accompanied by a long bar in the direction of the new trend. One can add that the chance of the gap being "filled" at the start of a new trend is not great.

For investors, such a Breakaway Gap is important because it is a powerful signal that a new trend is starting, and the gap is an early signal. This gap serves as a signal for investors to seriously consider exiting the positions of the previous trend if they have not yet done so, and to open a position in the new trend just starting!

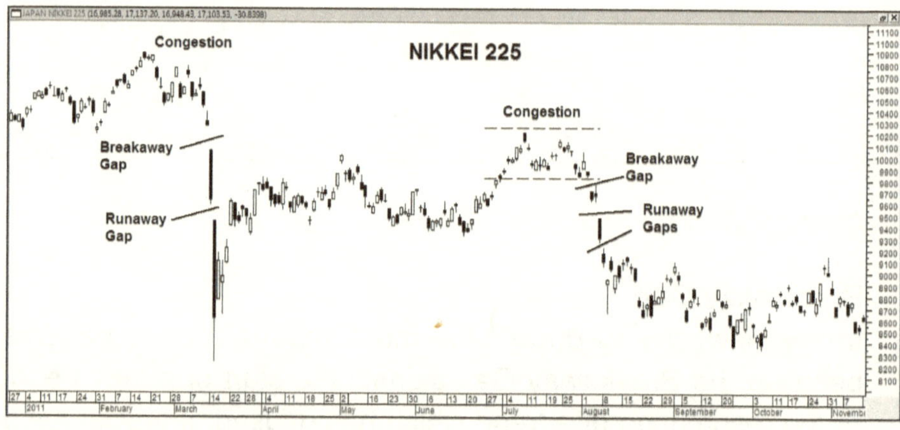

Chart 2.6: Breakaway Gap at the start of a downtrend and Runaway Gaps

A Breakaway Gap can also occur after a congestion, and the gap signals that the trend is resuming after the congestion.

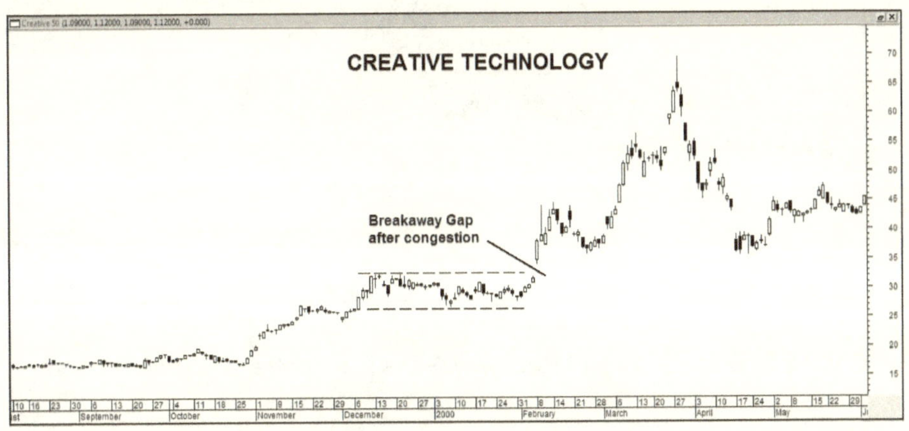

Chart 2.7: Breakaway Gap after a congestion in an uptrend

Other Indicators: For investors who use trendlines, the Breakaway Gap and its accompanying price bar should penetrate the trendline.

Runaway Gap

After a trend has started, and enters a fast-moving phase when price is falling or rising steeply, Runaway gaps appear. Runaway gaps are located between two vertically rising or falling bars, amidst large price movements over a few bars. In a rising market, they will typically be found between white candlesticks, and in a falling market, between black candlesticks. Runaway gaps are not frequently filled.

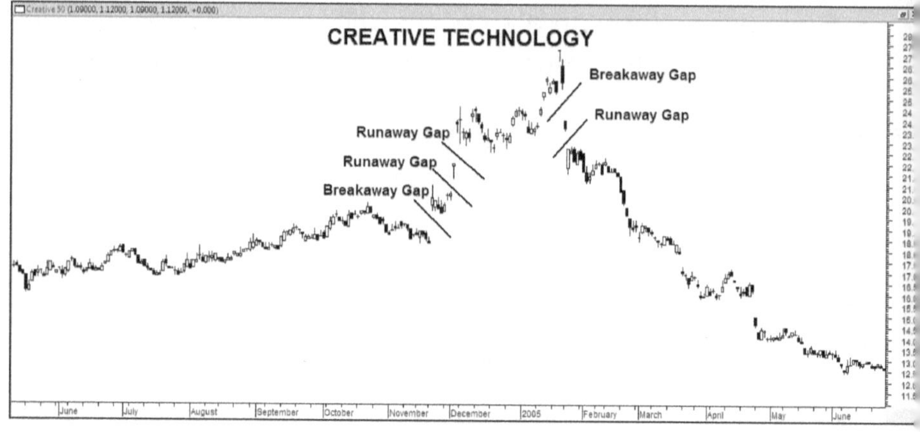

Chart 2.8: Breakaway and Runaway Gaps in an uptrend and downtrend

Key Reversal

This "price pattern" is one that reverses a trend on the basis of a single bar. The question that immediately arises in an investor's mind is - is it possible for just one bar to signal the change in a trend? Answer: it is possible, but extremely rare, and for a bar to qualify, the conditions have to be very stringent and must all be met.

Conditions for a Key Reversal

Firstly, there must have been a sizeable trend and a steep move, up or down.

Secondly, the potential Key Reversal has to be the highest or lowest bar of the trend so far. However, the bar not only has to be the highest or lowest bar thus far, but afterwards as well. If subsequently the market gets higher or lower, the suspected Key Reversal is invalidated.

Thirdly, the Key Reversal has to be an outside range bar; in other words it has a higher high, and lower low compared to the immediate bar before it. A similar high or similar low is not acceptable.

Finally, the Key Reversal's closing price has to be the reverse of the immediate previous bar; i.e. if it was an uptrend, the Key Reversal's closing price has to be LOWER than the previous bar's closing price. If it was a downtrend, the Key Reversal's closing price has to be HIGHER than the previous bar's closing price. A closing price that is similar to the previous bar is not acceptable.

Key Reversals can be a standalone bar that turns the trend in a dramatic fashion, or it can occur as part of another price pattern, say as the highest bar in other reversal patterns such as a double top or head-&-shoulders pattern.
The important point to remember about a potential Key Reversal is for the trader to be alert to the possibility of a Key Reversal as a market approaches dramatic highs or lows. Hence the investor has to be aware that it may occur, and should all 4 conditions seem to be met in one bar, then the investor can prepare for it to signal the change in trend.

However, if any of the conditions for the Key Reversal is breached, then the investor must accept that the signal is invalidated. And he resumes the search for the Key Reversal, if it is to happen at all.

Chart 2.9: Key Reversal top.

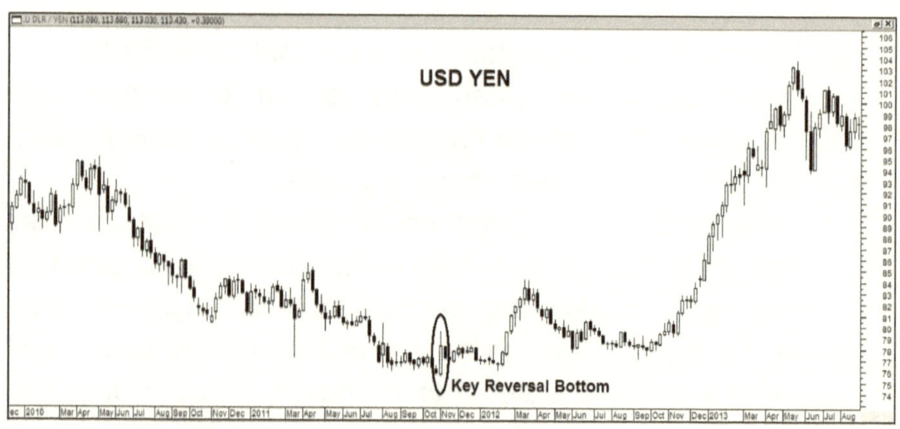

Chart 2.10: Key Reversal bottom.

Other Indicators: Do look out for a steep Breakaway Gap to follow the Key Reversal to increase the chance of the Key Reversal being valid.

DEFINING TREND WITH SELECTED CANDLESTICKS

On the whole, I tend to be selective about using Candlesticks and classical price patterns to forecast trend changes unless they occur with signals from other indicators. Standalone signals such as single bars suggesting market tops and bottoms may prove premature or subjective.

However, I do find that candlesticks are still effective in suggesting strength and weakness in a market, even though they may not turn the trend. So when such candlesticks are positioned at key positions in a chart, they can signal continued weakness or strength.

As such, my treatment of candlestick patterns here will be brief, and will highlight candlesticks which have proved useful in connection with other indicators such as moving averages, Bollinger Bands, price patterns, etc. But investors who wish to learn candlestick charting in greater depth are free to spend more time on them.[1]

Marubozu

These are long candlesticks without upper or lower shadows. They can be white or black candlesticks. Either way, the price action is a one-way movement from the opening price to the closing.

In the case of the white Marubozu, the price rises from the opening price, which is the low of the period, and closes at the

---

[1] Steve Nison, Japanese Candlestick Charting Techniques, Prentice Hall Press; 2 edition, November 1, 2001

high of the period. In the case of the black Marubozu, the reverse happens, and prices falls from the opening price, which is the high of the period, to the closing, which is the low of the period.

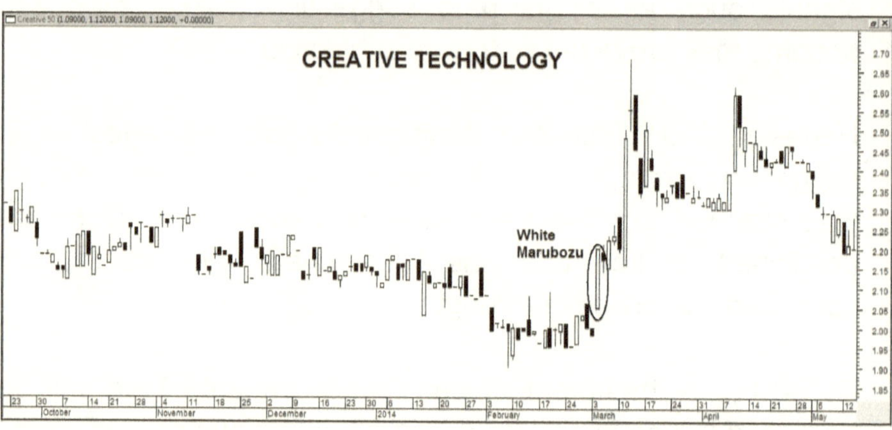

Chart 2.11: White Marubozu

Chart 2.12: Black Marubozu

20

The significance of the Marbozu lies in the length of the candlestick, the longer it is, the stronger is the move. The Marubozu which is positioned near other important signals such as after a breakaway gap, or after a reversal candlestick bar, will be a powerful signal of an impending significant move.

On the other hand a short candlestick, black or white, with or without shadows is usually not significant by itself. In other words, the black candlestick which is short does not mean that there is weakness thereafter; and a white candlestick which is short, does not mean that the market will definitely rise after it.

Long Lower Shadow

A candlestick with a long lower shadow signals that sellers initially dominate the session, but buyers subsequently force prices up to close the session higher. The longer the shadow, the more bullish the signal, and the market is expected to rise thereafter.

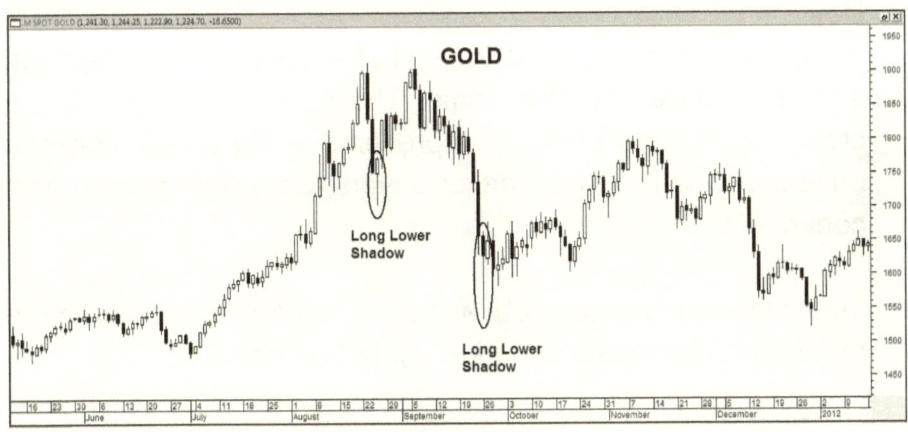

Chart 2.13: Candlestick with long lower shadow

Long Upper Shadow

This means that buyers initially dominate the session, but sellers later forced prices off the high to close the session lower. The longer the shadow, the more bearish is the signal, and the market is expected to decline thereafter.

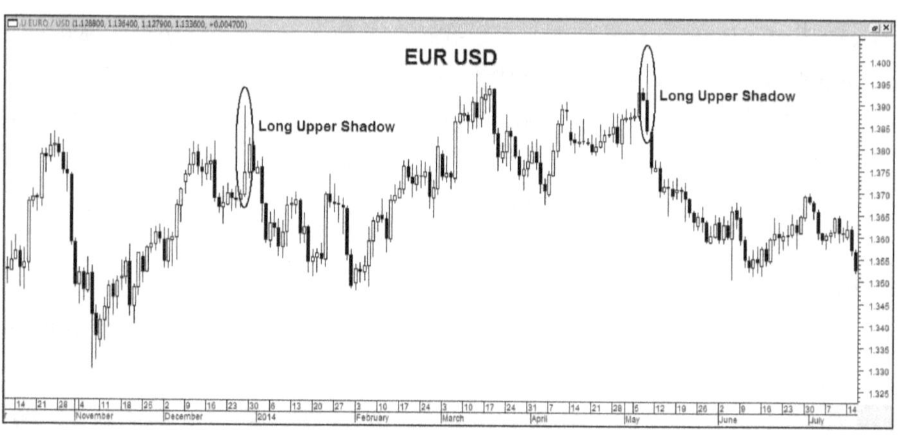

Chart 2.14: Candlestick with long upper shadow

Doji

A doji has a horizontal line instead of a real body; i.e. the open and close prices are the same. The candlestick looks like a cross, or inverted cross. It represents a tug-of-war between buyers and sellers with neither buyers nor sellers able to gain control of the market.

In a non-trending market, a doji is neutral. After a mature trend, a doji suggests a market top or bottom.

Chart 2.15: Doji Top

Chart 2.16: Doji bottom

Dragon Fly Doji & Gravestone Doji

These look like an ordinary Doji, opening and closing prices are the same – i.e. a "line" body, but they have a long lower shadow or upper shadow.

The Gravestone Doji has a long upper shadow and the body is also the low of the period. It is bearish.

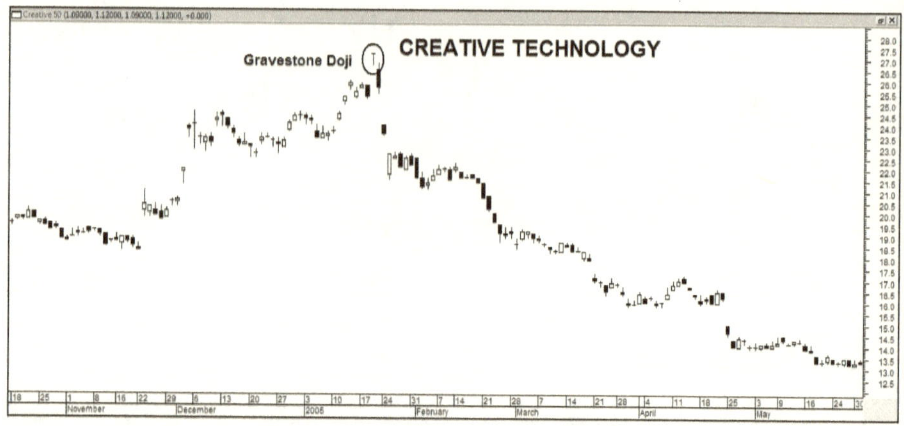

Chart 2.17: Gravestone Doji

The Dragonfly_Doji has a long lower shadow and the body is the high of the period. It is bullish.

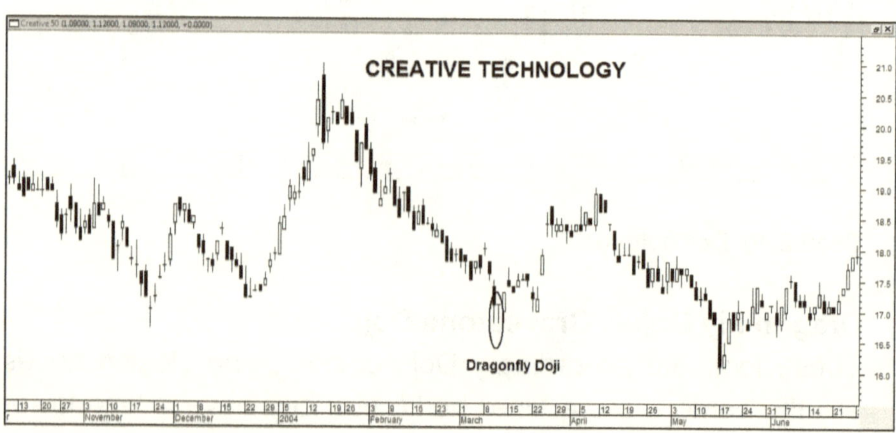

Chart 2.18: Dragonfly Doji

Bearish Reversal Patterns
Hanging Man

This candlestick has a small black body and long lower shadow. It is a bbearish reversal but a bearish confirmation such as a gap down or long black body thereafter on heavy volume provides a clearer signal.

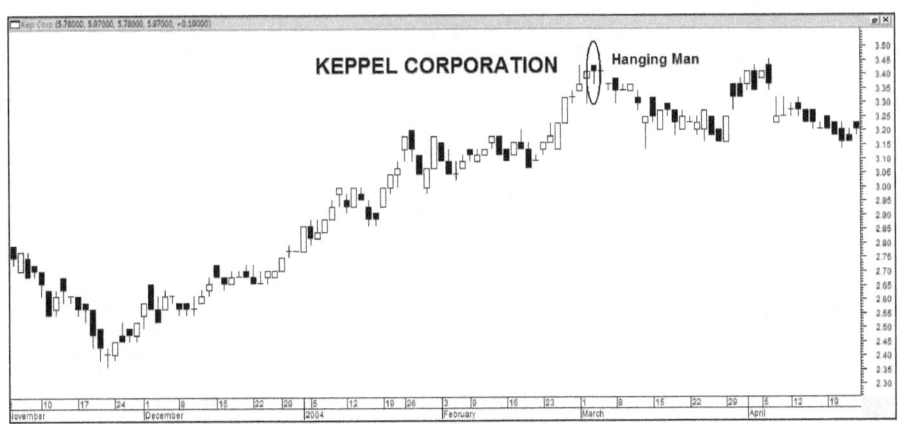

Chart 2.19: Hanging Man

Shooting Star

Small black body and a long upper shadow at least 2 times the length of the body. It is a bearish reversal, but confirmation is needed in the form of a gap or long black candlestick thereafter on heavy volume.

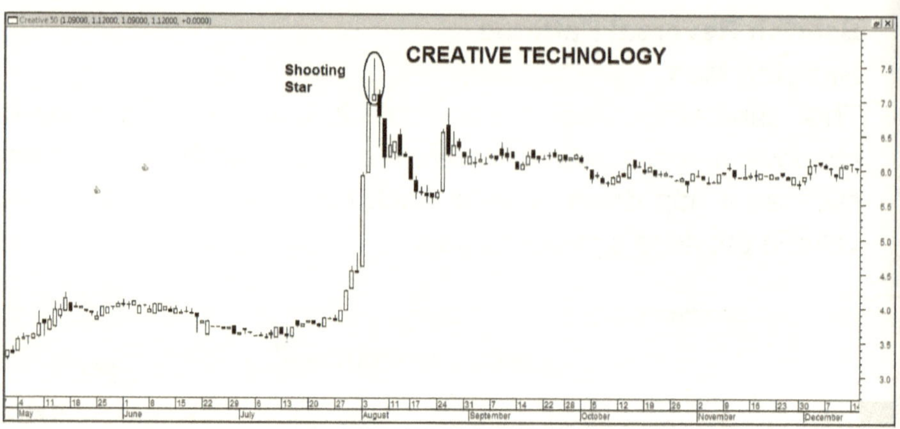

Chart 2.20: Shooting Star

Bullish Candlesticks
Hammer

A small white body and a long lower shadow at least 2 times the length of the body. The first bounce from a hammer may fail and the market may return to test the hammer's support.

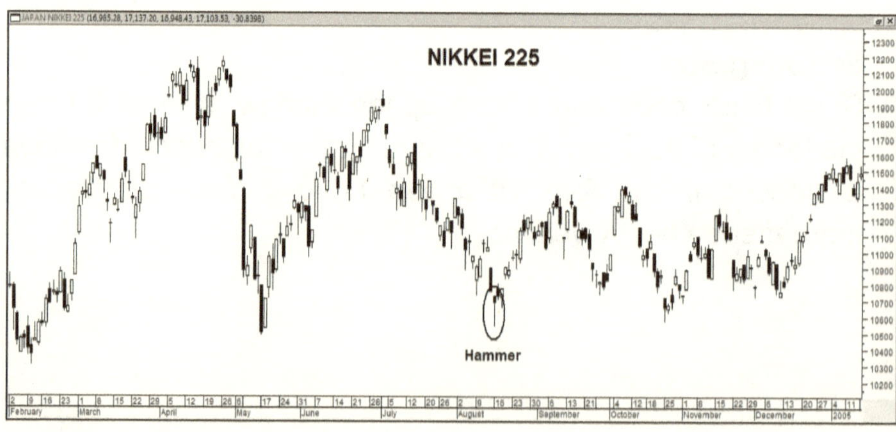

Chart 2.21: Hammer

Inverted Hammer

Looks exactly like a shooting star, but found in a market bottom instead and is a bullish pattern after a downtrend.

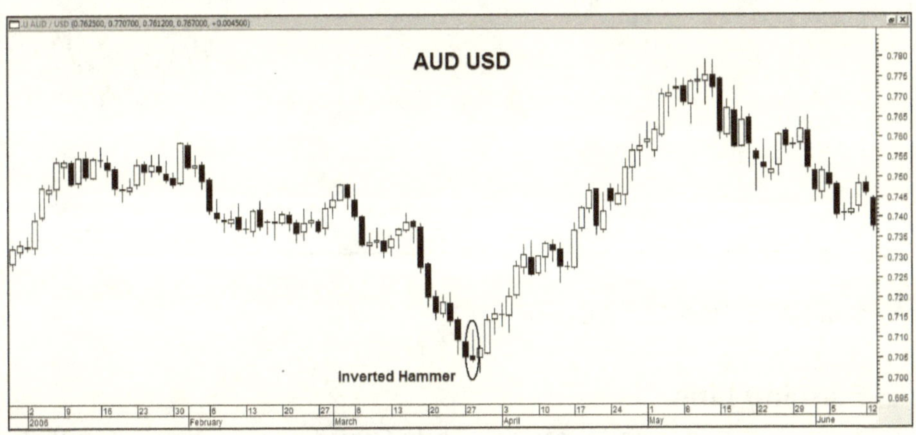

Chart 2.22: Inverted Hammer

Reversal Patterns

Dark Cloud Cover

This is a bearish pattern. After an uptrend, a long white candlestick is followed by a black candlestick. The black candle's closing price is at least BELOW the midpoint of the white candlestick.

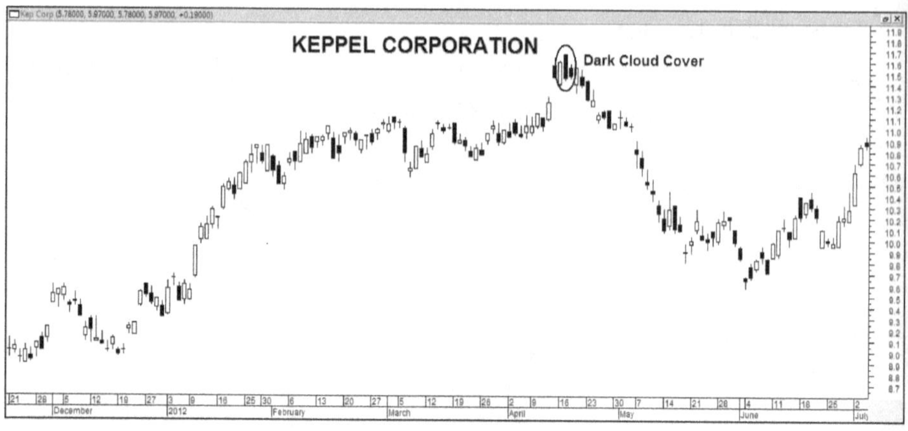

Chart 2.23: Dark Cloud Cover

Piercing Line

This is the opposite of the Dark Cloud Cover and is bullish. After a downtrend, a long black candlestick is followed by a white candlestick. The white candle's closing price is at least ABOVE the midpoint of the black candlestick.

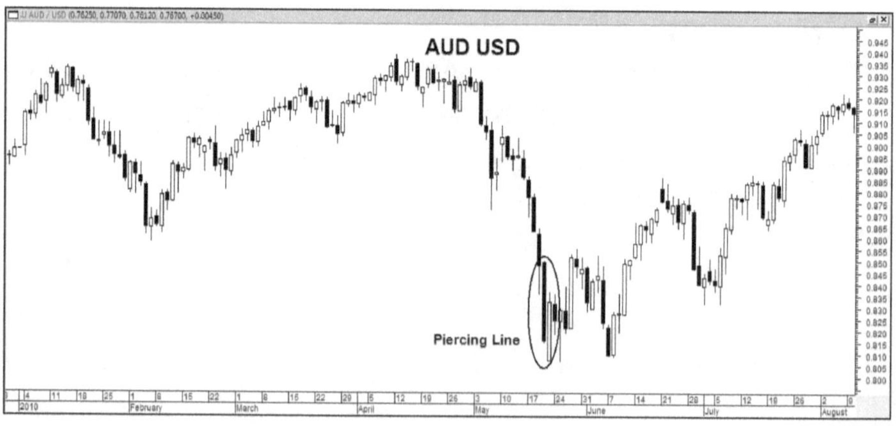

Chart 2.24: Piercing Line

Conclusion

Despite being a technician, trends are fundamentally driven, and they will turn over time with the changing fundaments. Hence I generally subscribe to technical indicators that signal a gradual turn in trend. Of course there will be times when markets turn sharply, but these tend to be less frequent.

Minor price patterns or candlesticks can effectively reflect shorter term reversals. They are useful for the technically-inclined investor to spot these minor turns in the market. I do suggest caution in using single bar or candlestick patterns to decide on a change in trend. Rather, if the price pattern is supported by broader technical signals of a change in trend, then the importance of the price pattern is enhanced. So it is with this perspective that I move to an important trend signal in the next chapter involving the 10 and 40 Exponential Moving Averages.

CHAPTER 3 - FORECASTING TREND WITH 10/40 EXPONENTIAL MOVING AVERAGES

Predicting the future!

Moving averages are among the oldest technical tools in the books, and most traders use some form of moving averages. I have used this particular combination of moving averages for a long time, and **this is the single most important single indicator in my toolbox because of its dual role in defining trend and in providing key support and resistance levels**. This combination of moving averages is also important for the same roles in the Time Frame Technique in Chapter 9 for managing long-term investment. In addition, this indicator has proved to be effective in many markets - stocks, indices, commodities, currencies and others.

Moving Average Basics

5-day Simple Moving Average Calculation

Date	Price Data	5-Day Total	5-Day **SMA**
March 4	95		
5	97		
6	96		
7	99		
8	101	488	97.6
11	103	496	99.2
12	104	503	100.6
13	106	513	102.6
14	108	522	104.4
15	106	527	105.4
18	103	527	105.4
19	104	527	105.4
20	100	521	104.2

When the Moving Average (MA) values are plotted, they form a line. When price is rising, the MA value/line rises; when price is falling, the MA value/line falls.

In a rising market, the MA line is situated <u>below price</u>, whereas in a falling market, the MA line is located <u>above price</u>.

Types of Moving Averages

There are 3 types of MA – simple, weighted and exponential moving average. They differ in the weightage attached to the latest price in their formulation. For simple moving average (SMA), all prices used in the formulation are given equal weight. For weighted moving average (WMA), the largest weight is assigned to the latest price. For exponential moving average (EMA), the weight assigned to the latest price is in between the extremes of SMA and WMA.

The outcome of the different weightages is that WMA values are closest to price, whereas SMA values are furthest from price even when calculated with the same prices. EMA values are generally in between the other two. When all three lines are plotted, the outcome is that the WMA line is closest to price; the SMA line is furthest from price, whereas the EMA line is in between. For optimal results, it is recommended that EMA be adopted when using MA as an indicator.

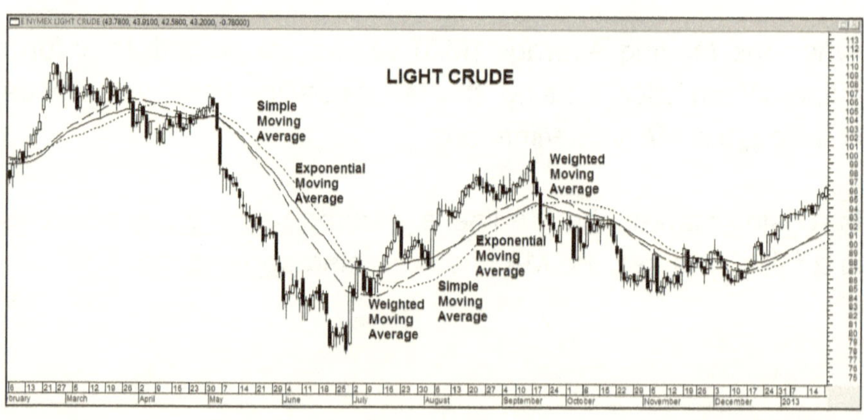

Chart 3.1: 40-day Simple, Weighted & Exponential Moving Averages

Number of Periods

The number of periods used in calculating MA is also important. The smaller the number, the closer is the line to the price, and vice versa. This is true whatever type of moving average used - WMA, SMA or EMA.

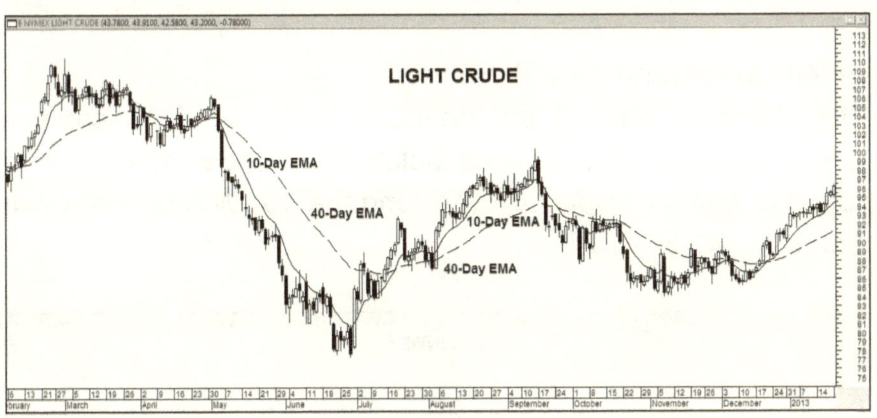

Chart 3.2: Effect of varying number of periods used in moving averages

Number of Moving Average lines

Technical analysts tend to use more than one MA to analyse markets. My basic MA combination consists of 2 lines, and for more than two decades I have found that the combination of 10 EMA and 40 EMA has proved to be an excellent tool.

Other MA lines can be added to provide more support or resistance levels and the number of periods can typically vary from 5 periods up to 200 periods. But for good measure, the 10 and 40 EMA combination has served me very well.

10/40 Exponential Moving Average Trend Signals

10/40 Uptrend Signal

An uptrend is defined as the point when the 10 EMA crosses above 40 EMA and remains above it. In an uptrend, price tends to remain above the 10 EMA, and the 10 EMA is positioned above the 40 EMA.

10/40 Downtrend Signal

Downtrend is defined as the point when 10 EMA crosses below 40 EMA and remains below it. In a downtrend, price tends to remain below 10 EMA, and the 10 EMA is positioned below the 40 EMA.

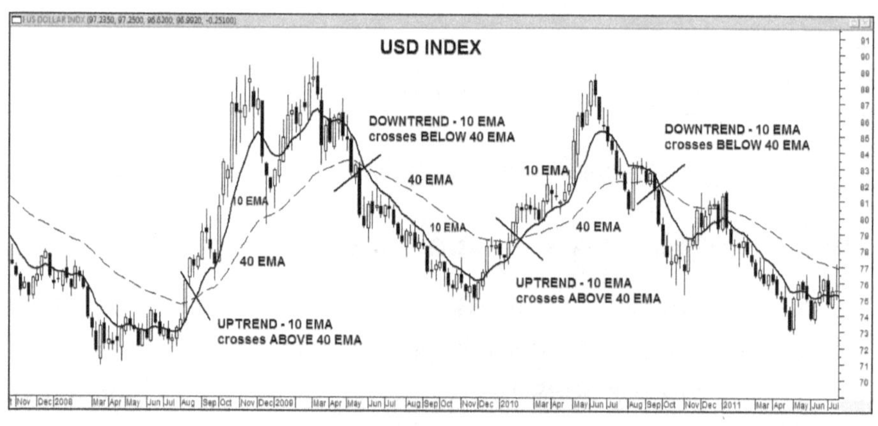

Chart 3.3: Uptrend & Downtrend as defined by 10 and 40 EMA

<u>Note</u>: It should be noted that the cross-over point of the 10 and 40 EMA is the point at which the trend changes. The meaning of "change in trend" is that the market's mood has changed – after the 10 EMA has crossed above 40 EMA, one can expect that price will have higher highs and lows, vice versa. 10 EMA crossing 40 EMA is NOT a timing signal to buy

or sell, as timing to buy or sell is provided by timing indicators such as Stochastics and Moving Average Convergence Divergence (MACD), which will be covered in later chapters.

3-Stage Process of 10/40 EMA Change in trend

Downtrend to uptrend

In a downtrend, when price rises and crosses above the 10 EMA, it should initially be viewed as a retracement. Should price then trade towards the 40 EMA, it should still be viewed as a deeper retracement.

However, should price finally break ABOVE and REMAIN above 40 EMA, then the downtrend may be turning up. As price initially crosses the 40 EMA, the 10 EMA will be pulled close to the 40 EMA. Eventually when price consistently remains above the 40 EMA, 10 EMA will finally cross 40 EMA, signalling the change to uptrend.

Uptrend to downtrend
The reverse happens.

In summary, the 3-stage process of a change in trend is as follows –
- Price crosses 10 EMA
- Price crosses 40 EMA
- 10 EMA crosses 40 EMA.

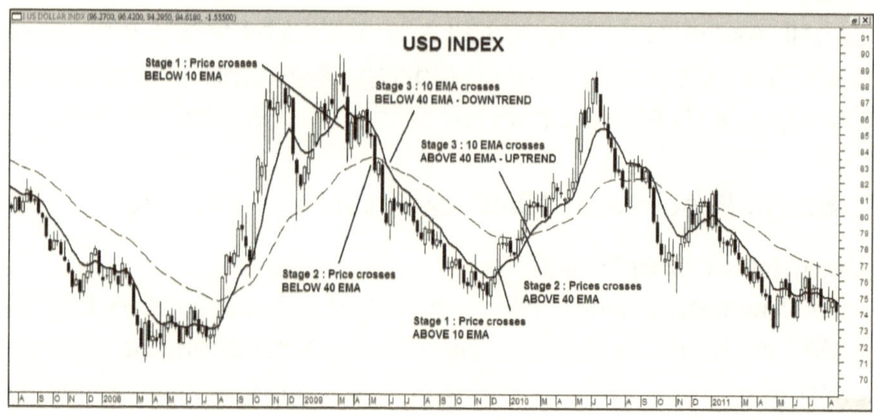

Chart 3.4: 3-stage process of 10/40 EMA change in trend

Importance of the 10/40 EMA Trend Signal

As simple as the above signal appears, it has worked as a powerful signal for a change in trend of all markets I have analysed, whether stocks, commodities, currencies, etc. Significantly, this signal also works for various time frames from the daily to the weekly, monthly charts and beyond. (See Chapter 9 on Time Frames.)

One could ask why this indicator works? The technical explanation for this signal to work maybe because the 10 EMA can be said to represent the short-term strength of market, whereas the 40 EMA represents the long-term strength. So if 10 EMA is greater than 40 EMA, then there is underlying strength in the market, i.e. uptrend. And vice versa.

10/40 Exponential Moving Averages as Support/Resistance in Trending Markets

The role that 10 and 40 EMA play as support in an uptrend and resistance in a downtrend is extremely important. This is in fact the second most important use of the 10/40 EMA combination. As in the 10/40 trend signal, the support/resistance roles of 10/40 EMA have been found to work in all markets and in all time frames.

In a trending market when price retraces, <u>10 EMA is first support/resistance</u> while <u>40 EMA is second support/resistance</u>.

If price breaks the 10 EMA, one can expect 40 EMA to be the next support/resistance. However, retracement to 40 EMA is a lot less frequent move compared to the retracement to 10 EMA. In fact in a strong trend, retracement often just stops at the 10 EMA.

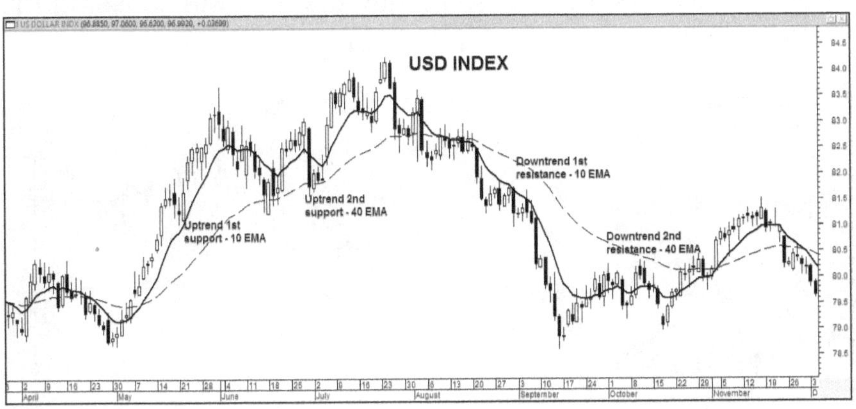

Chart 3.5: 10 EMA and 40 EMA as support/resistance in trending markets

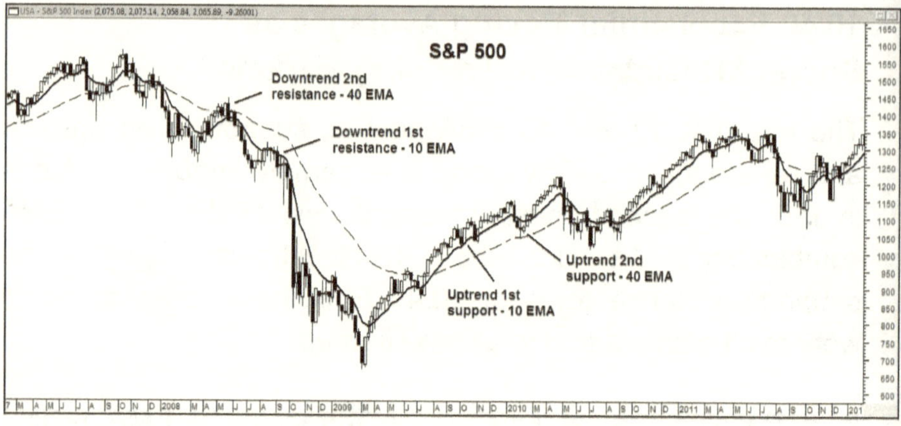

Chart 3.6: 10 EMA and 40 EMA as support/resistance in trending markets

Retracement to 40 Exponential Moving Average

In any major trend, it is common to have more than one retracement to the 40 EMA. So the first pullback to 40 EMA should not to be taken as a signal for a potential change in trend. However at the second move towards the 40 EMA, one can watch out for the possibility of price penetrating the 40 EMA line towards and subsequently the 10 EMA crossing the 40 EMA for the change in trend signal.

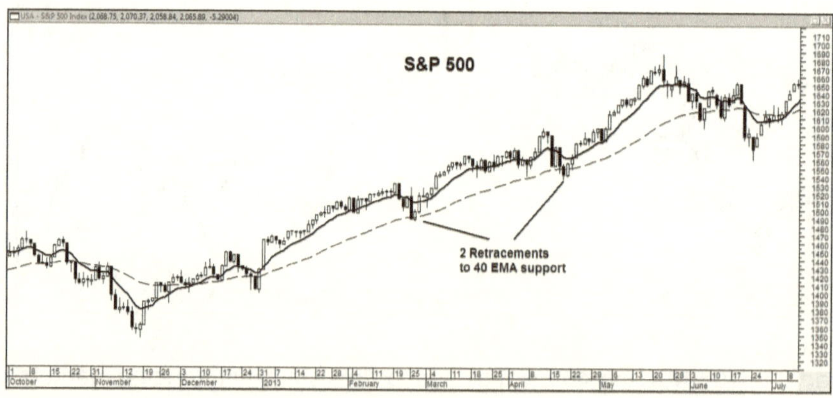

Chart 3.7: Two retracements to 40 EMA in Uptrend

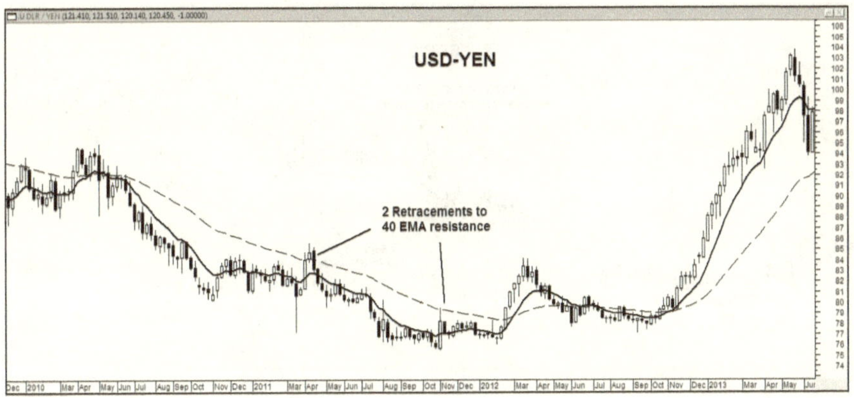

Chart 3.8: Two retracements to 40 EMA in Downtrend

Resumption of Trend Signal

At the end of a retracement to the 40EMA, the important signal to watch for is the resumption of the current trend by the price. In an uptrend, the resumption is represented by price trading back <u>above the 10 EMA</u>, an important signal of strength.

The same is true for the downtrend. At the end of the retracement up to the 40 EMA, if price falls back <u>below the 10 EMA</u>, it is a signal of the resumption of the downtrend.

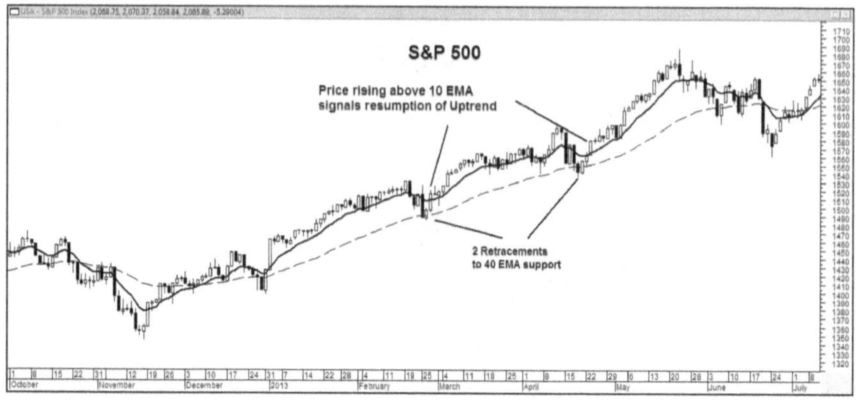

Chart 3.9: Resumption of uptrend when price rises above 10 EMA

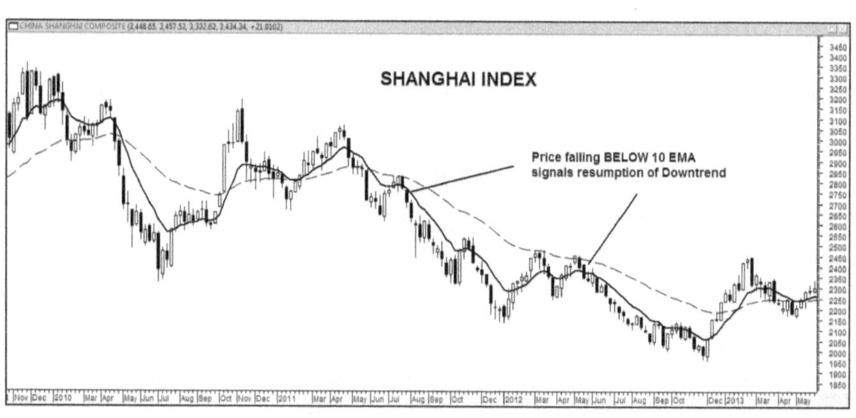

Chart 3.10: Resumption of downtrend when price falls below 10 EMA

The role of the 10 Exponential Moving Average in Strong Trends

If an uptrend is strong, price will remain firmly ABOVE the 10 EMA, and shallow corrections only bring it down to the 10 EMA. This situation happens in strong uptrends and can last for an extended period.

On the other hand, if the trend is down and market is weak, price will stay BELOW the 10 EMA and shallow corrections only bring it up to the 10 EMA. This situation happens in strong downtrends and can last for an extended period.

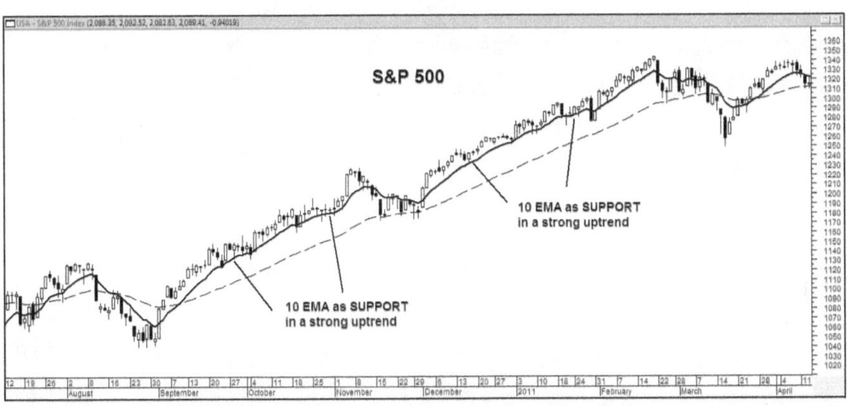

Chart 3.11: 10 EMA as support for an extended period in strong uptrend

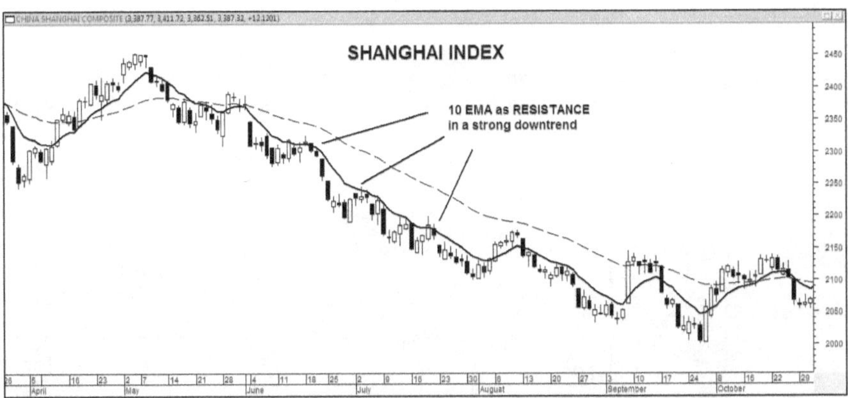

Chart 3.12: 10 EMA as resistance for an extended period in strong downtrend

10/40 Exponential Moving Averages in Congesting Markets

A congestion is easily recognised because 10 and 40 EMA criss-cross each other repeatedly.

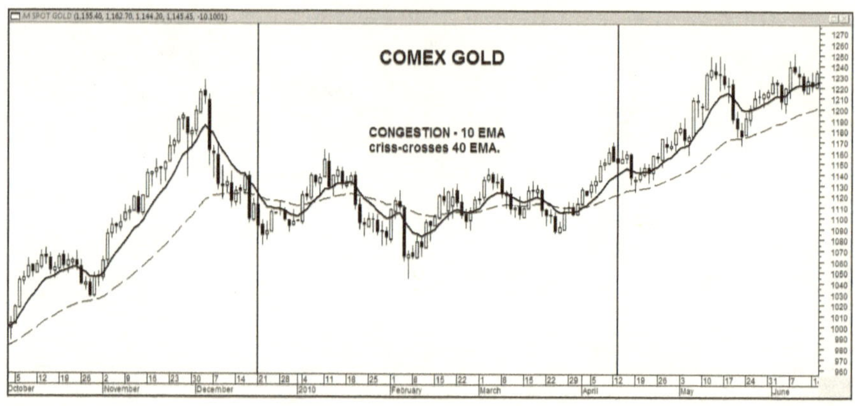

Chart 3.13: Congestion as indicated by 10 and 40 EMA criss-crossing each other

Chart 3.14: Congestion as indicated by 10 and 40 EMA criss-crossing each other

Similarly, in a congestion, 10 and 40 EMA do not play the role of support of resistance. This is true of all MA's, not just 10 and 40 EMA. Prices simply cut through MA lines during a congestion. In fact this characteristic can be used as the second signal for identifying a congestion.

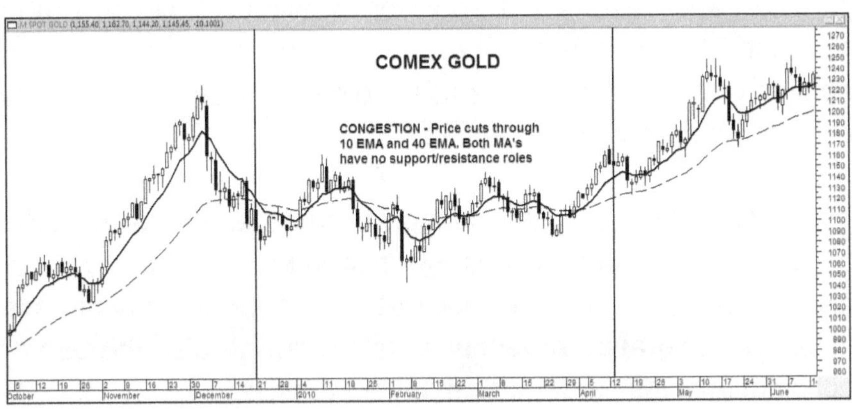

Chart 3.15: In a Congestion prices cut through 10 and 40 EMA

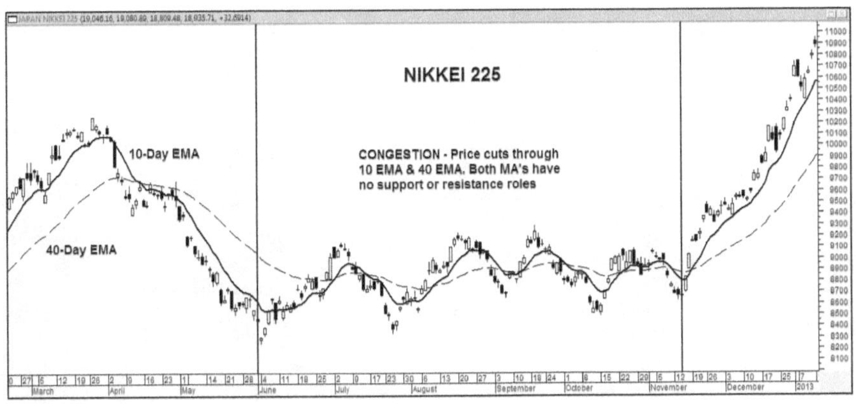

Chart 3.16: In a Congestion prices cut through 10 and 40 EMA

Other Indicators: Look for similar highs and lows in price action.

Conclusion

The simplicity but effectiveness of the 10/40 EMA as a trend indicator and also as a tool for arriving at support and resistance levels is not to be under-estimated. Investors can monitor the performance of this indicator in various markets and also in various time frames.

The 3-step process in the change in trend is also a powerful tool to follow a possible change in trend. The central role of this tool will return when we look at chapters 8 and 9 when we cover the integration of technical analysis and also the use of technical analysis for long-term investment.

CHAPTER 4 - PRICE TARGETS WITH BOLLINGER BANDS

Once you know it, you can't do without it!

This is an excellent and versatile indicator that can perform many useful functions for the investor. I have used it since the early 1990's when I discovered it by chance.

Bollinger Bands Formulation

Bollinger Bands have an elegant approach to creating an envelope based on the statistical tool of standard deviation.

Mid Band - 20 SMA.
Upper & Lower Bands - 2 standard deviation (SD) from 20 SMA.

According to statistical principles,
With 1 SD from the 20 SMA, the Upper and Lower Bands cover 66% of price bars;
With 2 SD from the 20 SMA, the Upper and Lower Bands cover 95% of price bars;
With 3 SD from the 20 SMA, the Upper and Lower Bands cover 99% of price bars.

The default Bollinger Bands formulation uses 2 SD, which produces an optimal result, i.e. only 5% of the bars will be outside of the Bands. This means that

(a) when price bars trade outside of the Bands, they only stay out minimally, only 5% of the time. There is pressure for the price bars to return into the Bands.
(b) under certain circumstances, the Upper and Lower Bands act as good support and resistance levels.

With 1 SD, the Bands end up being too narrow, and the price bars tend to stay outside of the Bands for much of the time.

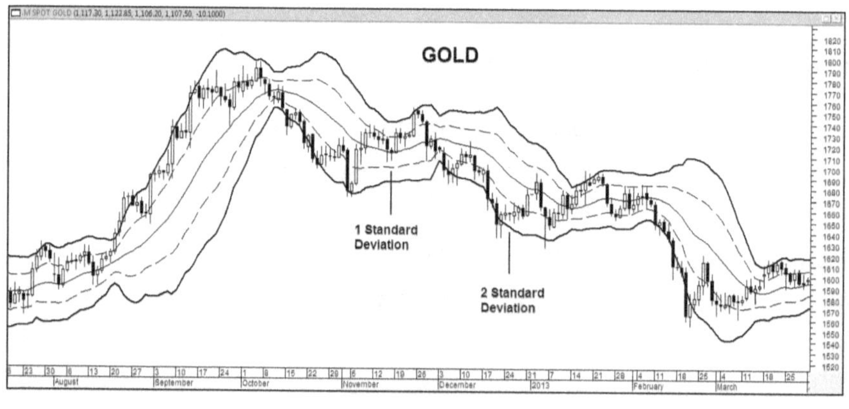

Chart 4.1: Bollinger Band with 1 Standard Deviation (black) and 2 Standard Deviation (blue)

With 3 SD, the Bands become very wide, and the price bars do not reach the Upper and Lower Bands or trade outside. This gives rise to a few useful signals.

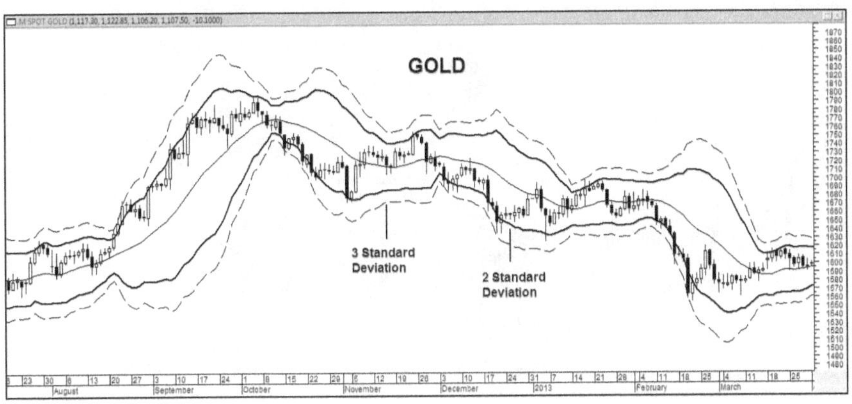

Chart 4.2: Bollinger Band with 3 Standard Deviation (red) and 2 Standard Deviation (blue)

Bollinger Bands applications in a Congestion

There are two extremely useful signals from Bollinger Bands during a congestion which are not offered by other indicators:

(a) Support & resistance - the Upper and Lower Bands are generally horizontal and they play the role of resistance and support quite well. In other words, price bars tend to stop falling around the Lower Band where the investor may use it as a buy level. On the other hand, around the Upper Band, price bars tend to turn down, and the investor may use the Upper Band as a sell level.

It should be noted that prices do not consistently reach either Band. When price does reach either Band, there may be intra-day penetration, but the chance of the bar resuming inside the Band is good. That often signals the turning point.

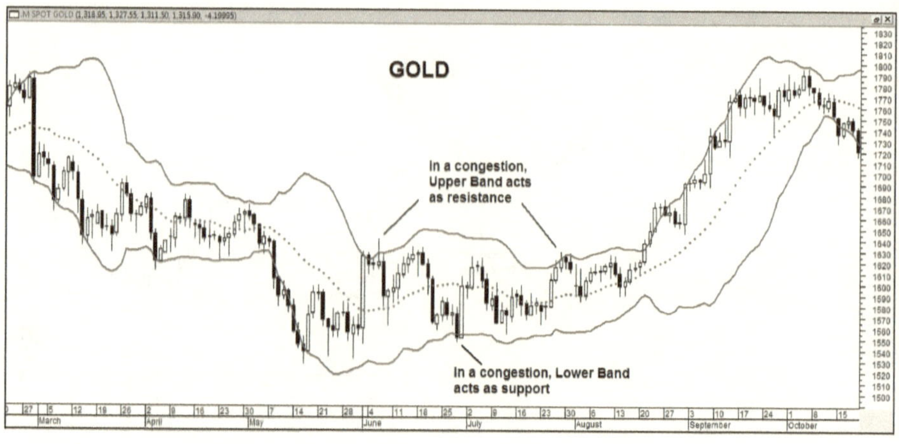

Chart 4.3: In a congestion, Upper and Lower Bands play the roles of resistance and support respectively

In Chapter 3 (10/40 EMA), we mentioned that MA's do not function as support/resistance during a congestion. The Mid Band here suffers from the same deficiency as it is only a 20 SMA. Price bars slice through them.

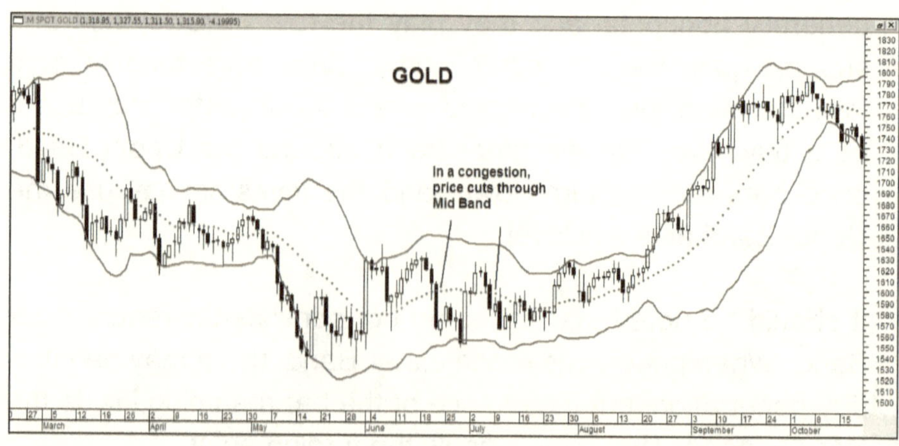

Chart 4.4: In a congestion, price cuts through Mid Band

(b) "Constriction" & Breakout - When price trades progressively into a narrow range in a congestion, it can draw both the Upper and Lower Bands together into tight squeeze, which I term a "constriction". When such a constriction occurs, it acts as a warning of the possibility of a breakout of the market from the congestion into a trending move. The 'tighter the constriction', the more dramatic is the breakout when it happens. Hence as a market congests, it is important to watch if the Bollinger Bands forms a constriction.

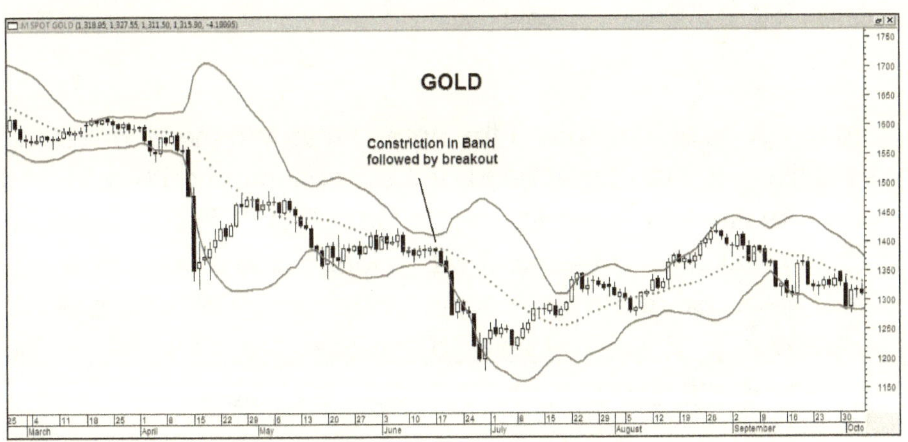

Chart 4.5: Constriction in Bollinger Band followed by a breakout in Gold

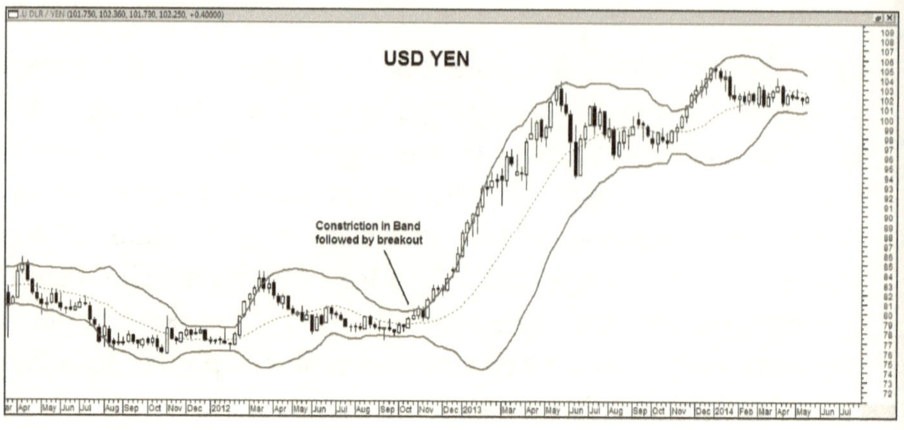

Chart 4.6: Constriction in Bollinger Band followed by a breakout in USD-YEN

At the point of breakout, if the price drives into the Upper Band it is likely to start an uptrend. If it pushes into the Lower Band the breakout is likely to start a downtrend. There could be false breaks, but a breakout with a long bar is a surer sign of a real breakout, and a surer sign of the direction of the breakout. However <u>it is not possible to forecast the direction of the breakout with Bollinger Bands prior to the breakout.</u>

It should be noted that a constriction is not a frequent occurrence. In fact, it is an uncommon occurrence, and investors have to learn to judge what constitutes a "constriction". But when it happens it is a powerful signal to warn of a breakout BEFORE it happens. On the other hand, it should be noted that markets do change from a congestion to trend without the drama and help of a band constriction.

Bollinger Bands applications in a Trending Market

When a market breaks out into a trend, the bands open up and the width or vertical distance of the Band increases. This opening of the band is especially dramatic after a constriction and remains until the move comes to an end.

There are several very useful features of the Band which investors should learn about and bear in mind.

(a) Price trading "along" the Band
If the breakout leads to an uptrend, price will trade along or ON the Upper Band. Unlike the congesting market, Upper Band does not function as resistance in a trend. If the breakout leads to a downtrend, the Lower Band does not function as support, and price will trade along or ON the Lower Band. When price is trading "along" either Band, <u>it signals that the trend will continue</u>.

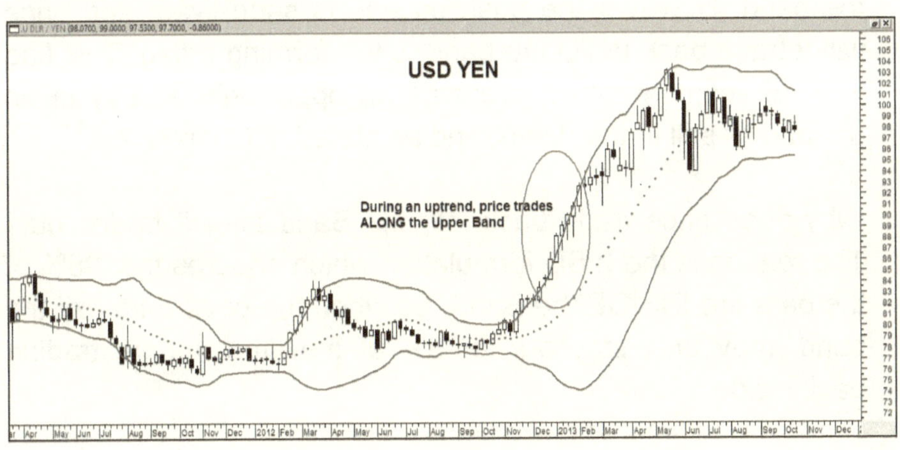

Chart 4.7: Price trading "along" the Upper Band in an uptrend

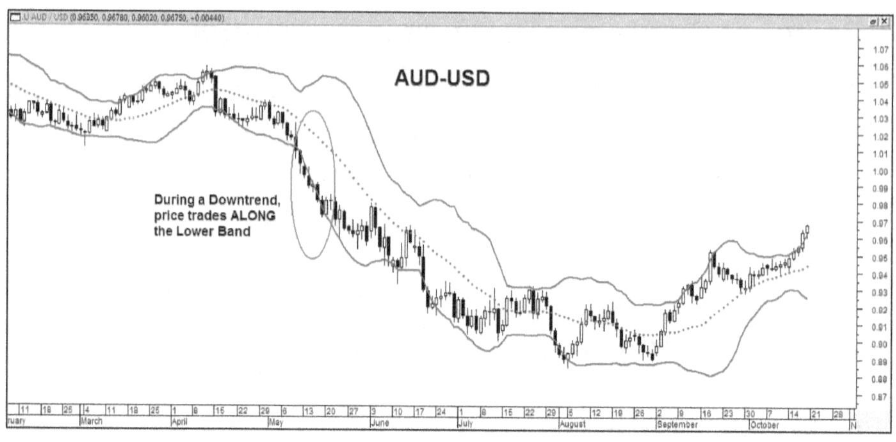

Chart 4.8: Price trading "along" the Lower Band in a downtrend

(b) Price "out" of the Band

There are times in a trending market when price surges and trades OUTSIDE of the bands, in both uptrend and downtrend. The surge will cause price to trade outside of the Upper Band – it can be one or two bars positioned completely outside of the band. However the push outside is short-lived, and price will retrace back INTO the band, often forming a flag. This flag is a retracement which presents an opportunity to buy in an uptrend or sell in the downtrend as stated in Chapter 2.

Why does price trade back into the Band after it trades out? The reason is the 2 SD formulation which ensures that 95% of the bars are INSIDE the Band. So when the price bars exit the band, they only stay out for 5% of the time, before trading back inside.

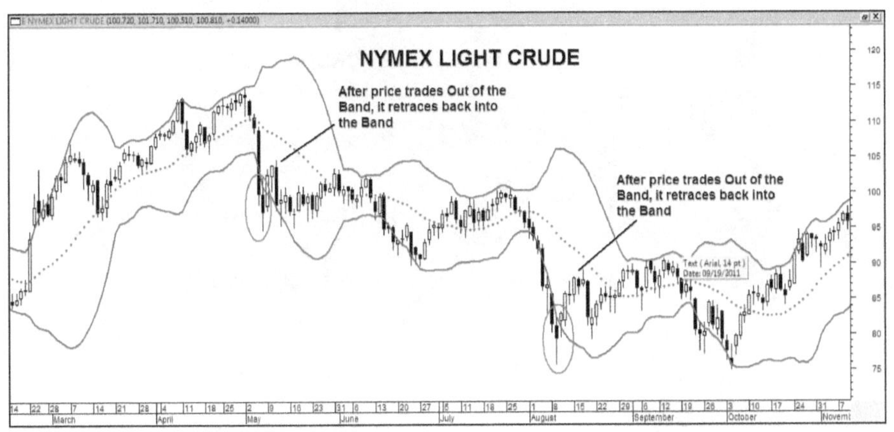

Chart 4.9: After trading "out" of the Band, prices retraces back INTO the Band

(c) Retracement Objective at Mid Band

After price goes out of the Band, the retracement move reaches one of 2 indicators, the 10 EMA or the Mid Band. If the trend is strong, then the retracement will be shallow and the flag will be supported by the 10 EMA. If the trend is not strong, the retracement is deeper, and price may reach the Mid Band, though it should be noted that retracement to the Mid Band occurs less frequently.

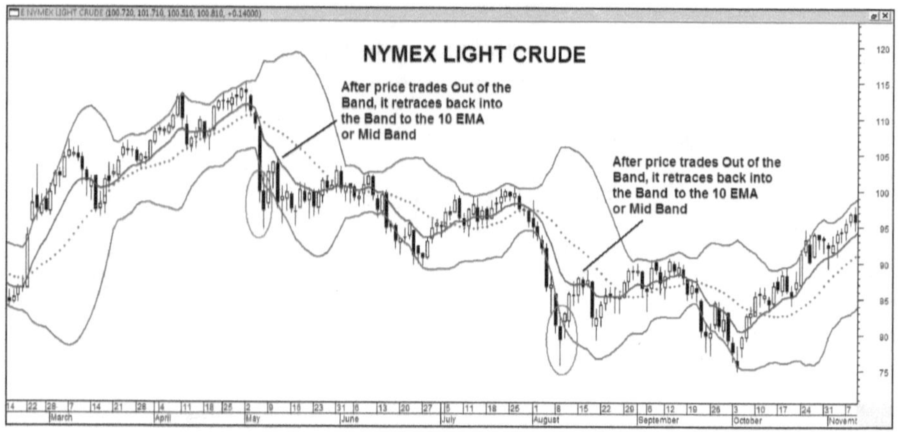

Chart 4.10: After trading "out" of the Band, prices retraces INTO the band towards the 10 EMA or Mid Band

<u>Important</u> : It should be pointed out that should price "retrace" past the Mid Band to reach the Lower Band in the uptrend, or Upper Band in the downtrend, then it may imply that the market is no longer in a retracement mode. A deeper move like that suggests that the original trending move is over and the market is entering into a congestion, or the market may even see a sudden trend reversal.

Bollinger Bands applications at the End of a Trend

(a) Bollinger Bands "Rounded top or bottom"
Another very useful signal from Bollinger Bands is its unique "rounding off" action as a trend slows down. In an uptrend, the Upper Band forming forms a "rounded top" as price slows down and trades sideways. This "rounded top" serves as a visual signal to investors that the previous uptrend is slowing down.

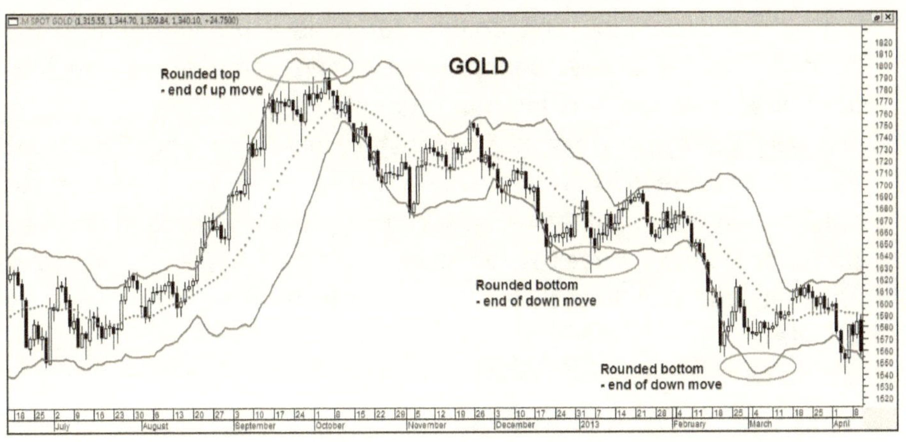

Chart 4.11: Rounded Top and Bottom signal the end of up move and down move

In a downtrend, the opposite occurs; the Lower Band forms a "rounded bottom" as the price slows down and trades sideways. This "rounded bottom" serves as a visual signal that the previous downtrend is slowing down.

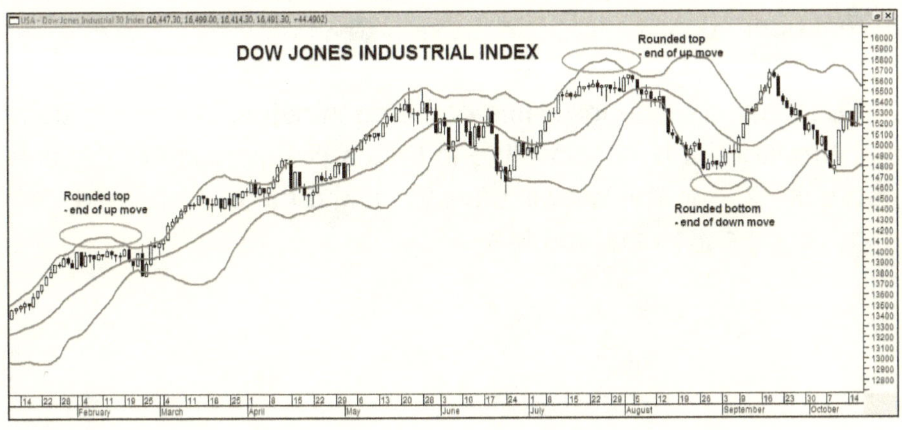

Chart 4.12: Rounded Top and Bottom signal the end of up move and down move

Both the rounded top and bottom serve as a broad signal to the investor that he should consider liquidating some of his previous positions. However, it is important to note <u>that this slowing down of the previous move does not necessarily mean its end</u>. The trend can still resume AFTER a rounded top or bottom - price can still breakout in the same direction of the previous trend. However, Bollinger Bands by itself is not able to indicate the end of a trend. For that, one has to look for the 10/40 EMA crossing signal (see Chapter 3).

Bollinger Bands Constraints

Despite the unique value of the Bollinger Bands to the investor, we should recognise two constraints in the indicator.

One is that strictly speaking it is not to be confused with 10/40 EMA as a trend indicator. There is no signal from Bollinger Bands to tell us a market's trend. In fact its benefits only accrue to us when we know a market's trend. Once we know that, we begin to look for the relevant signals from the Bands that benefit us.

Secondly, despite the value of the constriction in warning us of a breakout, it is not possible to tell us the direction of the final breakout. For that we will have to look to the overall trend from the price action and the MA's.

Conclusion

It should be clear to the investor that Bollinger Bands provides some very unique signals that helps the investor in ways that few other indicators can – the constriction of the Bands, the support and resistance levels during a congestions, price trading "out" of the band, and the rounded top and bottom, among others. There are still other secondary benefits from the Bands, but it is sufficient at this stage to know that it is an indicator that is an important part of the investor's toolbox – "once you know it, you can't do without it!"

CHAPTER 5 - PRICE TARGETS WITH FIBONACCI RATIOS

Unique Objective-setting method that works!

In the previous chapters on price, we covered indicators which can be used to arrive at support and resistance levels, levels to buy or sell at. The 10/40 EMA, and Bollinger Bands are two of such good methods.

The Fibonacci objective setting is another method which is used by technical analysts to arrive at support or resistance levels. This is a mathematical approach and has its origins in a series of numbers called Fibonacci numbers. This method is unique and unrelated to the moving averages and Bollinger Bands, but Fibonacci ratios can produce extremely valid price levels for the markets. At times they even coincide with moving averages and Bollinger Bands. In a word, Fibonacci objective setting methods is an important tool for arriving at key price levels, and a must for the investor's tool box.

Fibonacci Basics

Fibonacci Numbers

Fibonacci numbers were named after an Italian mathematician Leonard Fibonacci who wrote about the numbers in a book in 1202. The numbers are as follows -

0, 1, 1, 2, 3, 5, 8, 13, 21, 34, 55, 89, 144, 233, ...

These numbers are the created by summing up the first two numbers to produce the next number, and the process is then repeated to produce more numbers.

Fibonacci Ratios

From the numbers, a number of ratios are derived, and they are the result of using the series of numbers in different combinations. It should be noted that if the early numbers of the series are used, (1, 2, 3, 5, and 8), they do not produce the typical Fibonacci ratios. But as the progressively larger numbers are used, they will consistently end up with the Fibonacci ratios.

Ratio 0.382 = 34/89, 55/144, 89/233, etc

The ratio 0.382 is created by taking any one number from 13 onwards and dividing it by the SECOND number after it, in this case by 34.

Ratio 0.618 = 34/55, 55/89, 89/144, etc

The ratio 0.618 is created by taking any one number from 21 onwards and dividing it by the NEXT larger number after it, ie 34.

Ratio 1.618 = 55/34, 89/55, 144/89

The ratio 1.618 is created by taking any one number from 55 onwards and dividing it by the SMALLER number just before it, in this case 34.

The ratios 0.5 and 1.0 are produced by using the first 3 numbers, 1, 1, 2.

Fibonacci Ratios for Objective-setting

Retracement Ratios:	0.382
	0.5
	0.618
Expansion Ratios:	0.618
	1.0
	1.618

Retracement Projections

(a) Pick a prominent high point and prominent low point. These have to be the highest high of the move selected as well as the lowest low of the move. The gap between these two points represents the height (AB) of the move.

(b) Apply the 3 retracement ratios (0.382, 0.5 and 0.618) to the height to arrive at 3 possible retracement possibilities for a retracement move.

(c) In an uptrend, to arrive at a retracement DOWN objective, project the 3 retracement moves <u>down</u> from the HIGH point of the height to arrive at the retracement objectives.

(d) In a downtrend, to arrive at a retracement UP objective, project the 3 retracement moves <u>up</u> from the LOW point of the height to arrive at the retracement objectives.

RETRACEMENT PROJECTIONS

In a Downtrend,

In an Uptrend,

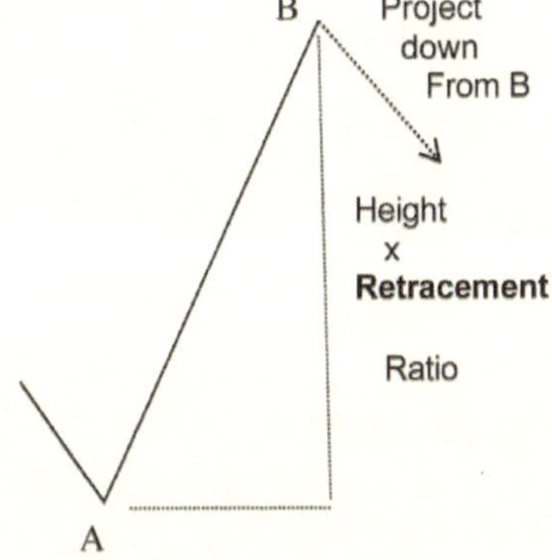

Figure 1: RETRACEMENT **UP**   Figure 2: RETRACEMENT **DOWN**

In a Downtrend,

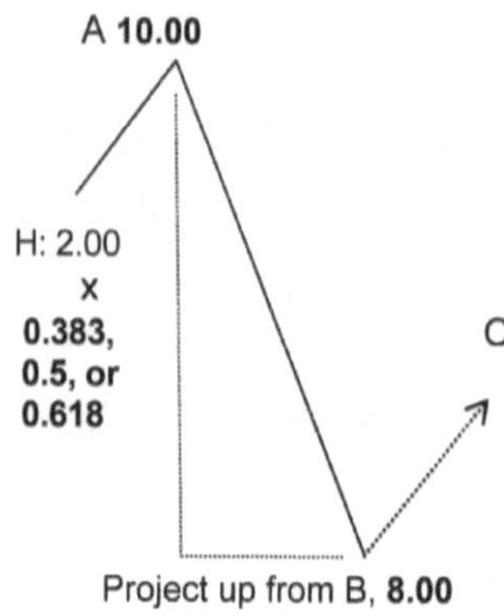

Figure 3

In an Uptrend,

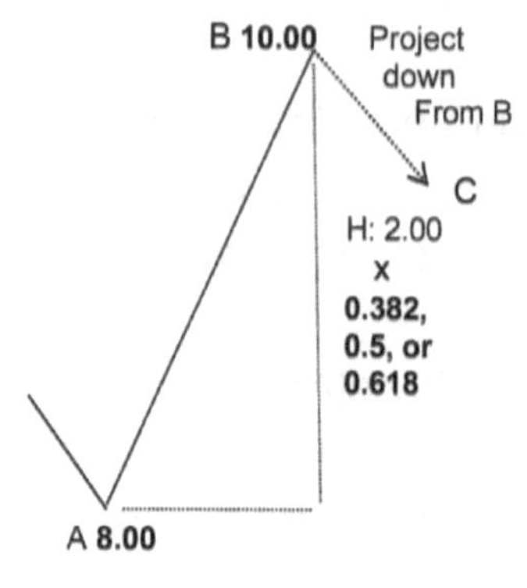

Figure 4

Calculation

0.382 Retracement UP

Height 2.00 x 0.382 = 0.76

Objv: 8.00 + 0.76

= 8.76

0.5 Retracement UP

Height 2.00 x 0.5 =1.00

Objv: 8.00 + 1.00

= 9.00

Calculation

0.382 Retracement DOWN

Height 2.00 x 0.382 = 0.76

Objv: 10.00 - 0.76

= 9.24

0.5 Retracement DOWN

Height 2.00 x 0.5 = 1.00

Objv: 10.00 - 1.00

= 9.00

0.618 Retracement UP

Height 2.00 x 0.618 = 1.24

Objv: 8.00 **+** 1.24

$\qquad$ = 9.24

0.610 Retracement DOWN

Height 2.00 x 0.618 = 1.24

Objv: 10.00 **-** 1.24

$\qquad$ = 8.76

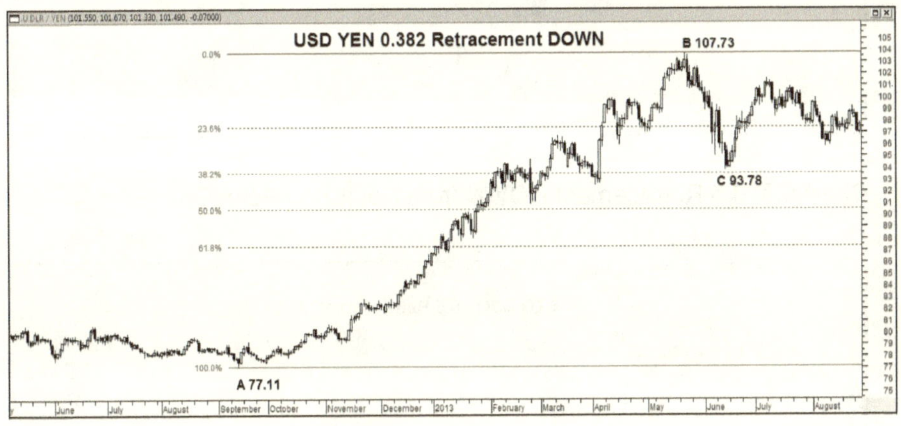

Chart 5.1: 0.382 Retracement DOWN from Point B to Point C

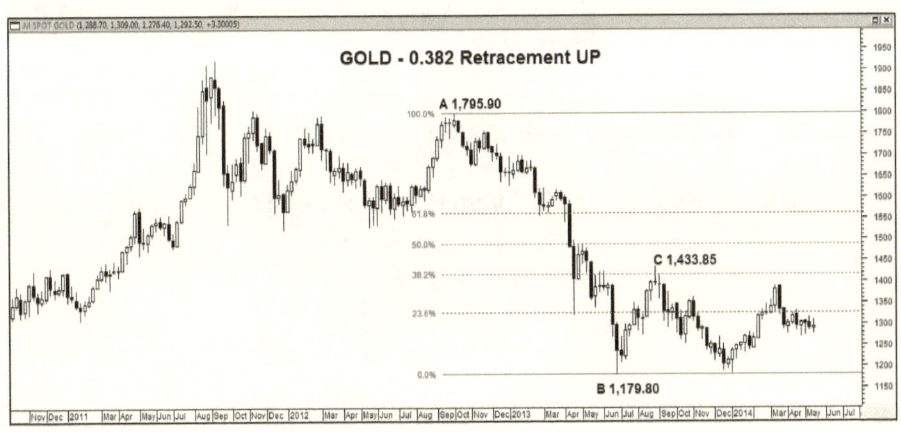

Chart 5.2: 0.382 Retracement UP from Point B to Point C

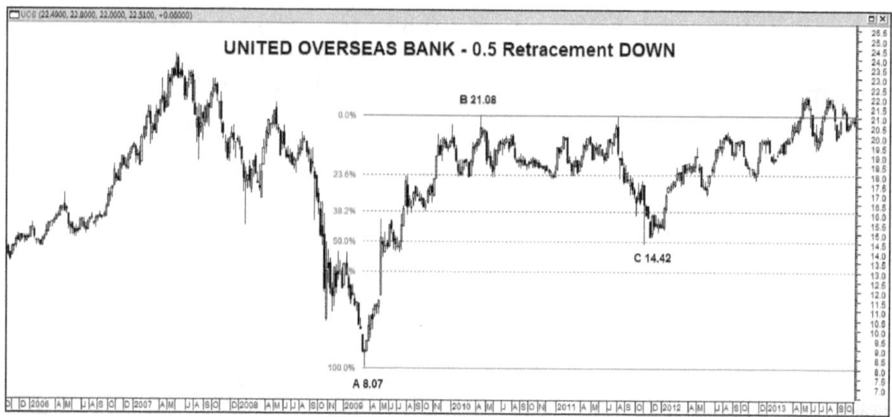

Chart 5.3: 0.5 Retracement DOWN from Point B to Point C

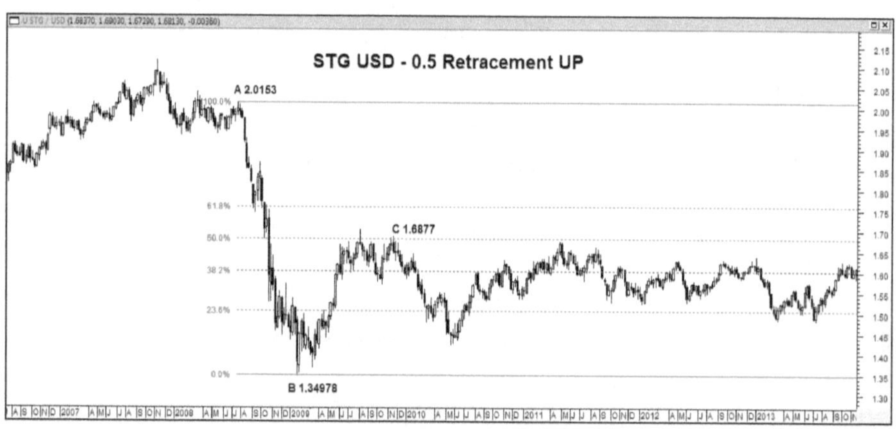

Chart 5.4: 0.5 Retracement UP from Point B to Point C

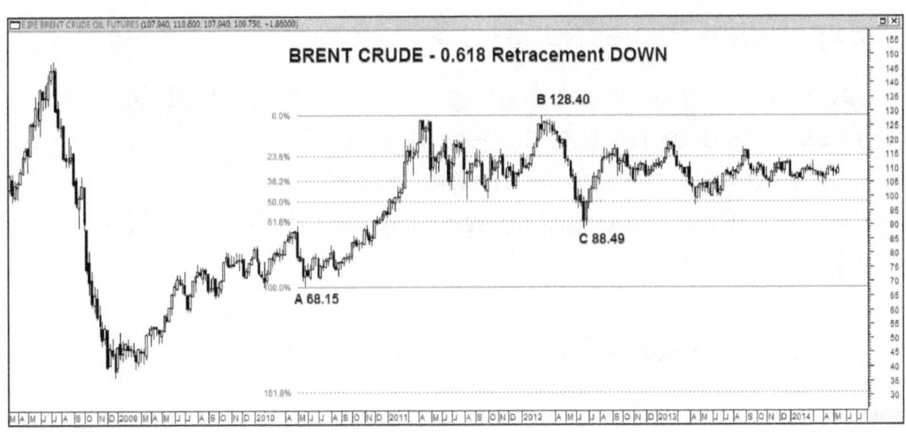

Chart 5.5: 0.618 Retracement DOWN from Point B to Point C

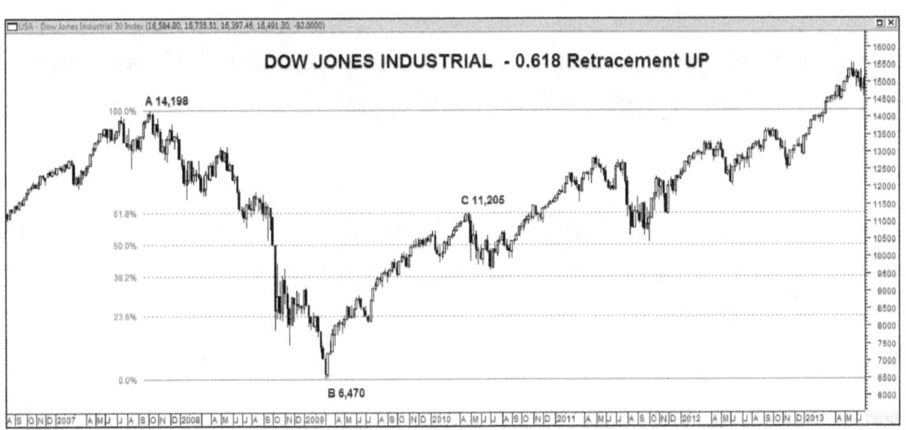

Chart 5.6: 0.618 Retracement UP from Point B to Point C

Expansion Projections

(a) Pick a prominent high point and prominent low point. These have to be the highest high of the move selected as well as the lowest low of the move respectively. The price gap between these two points represents the height (AB) of the move.

(b) Select a third point C, which is the retracement high or low <u>AFTER the height is selected</u>.

(b) Apply the 3 expansion ratios (0.618, 1.0 & 1.618) to the height to arrive at 3 possibilities for expansion.

(c) For an uptrend, to arrive at the expansion UP objectives, project the <u>3 moves up from point C</u>, and arrive at the objectives.

(d) For a downtrend, to arrive at a expansion DOWN objectives, <u>project the 3 moves down from point C</u>, and arrive at the objectives.

EXPANSION PROJECTIONS

In a Downtrend, expansion **DOWN**

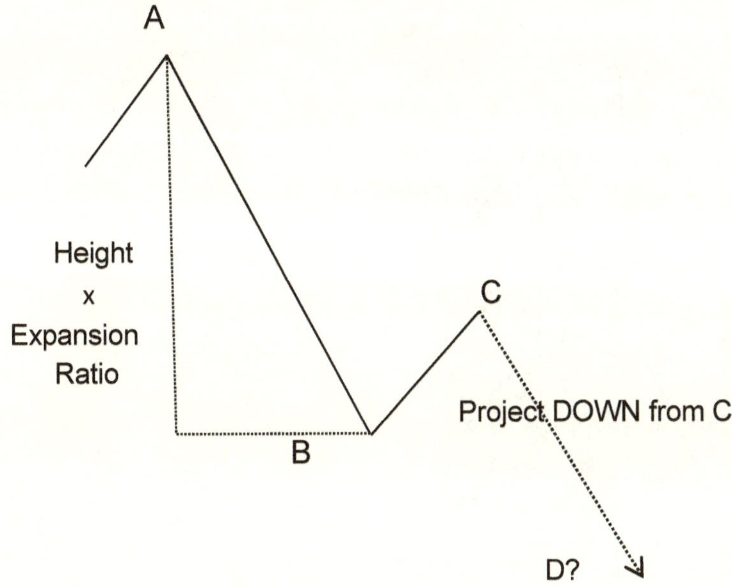

Figure 5

In an Uptrend, expansion **UP**

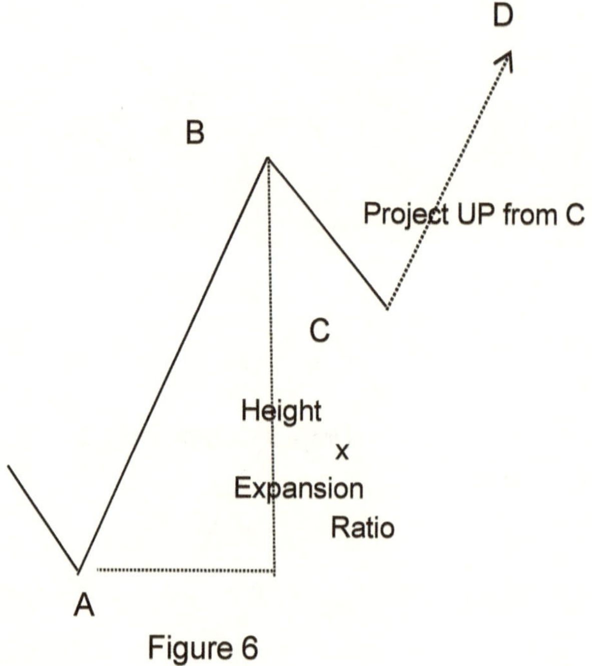

Figure 6

In a Downtrend,

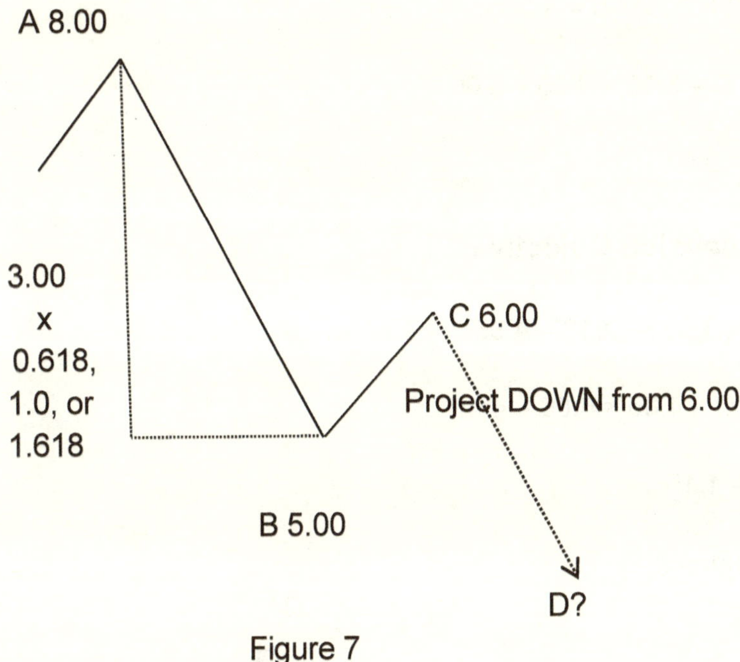

Figure 7

1st Expansion Objective

Height 3.00 x 0.618 = 1.85

Objv : C – 1.85 = 6.00 – 1.85

= 4.15

2nd Expansion Objective

Height 3.00 x 1.0 = 3.00

Objv: C – 3.00 = 6.00 – 3.00

= 3.00

3rd Expansion Objective

Height 3.00 x 1.618 = 4.85

Objv: C – 4.85 = 6.00 – 4.85

= 1.15

In an Uptrend,

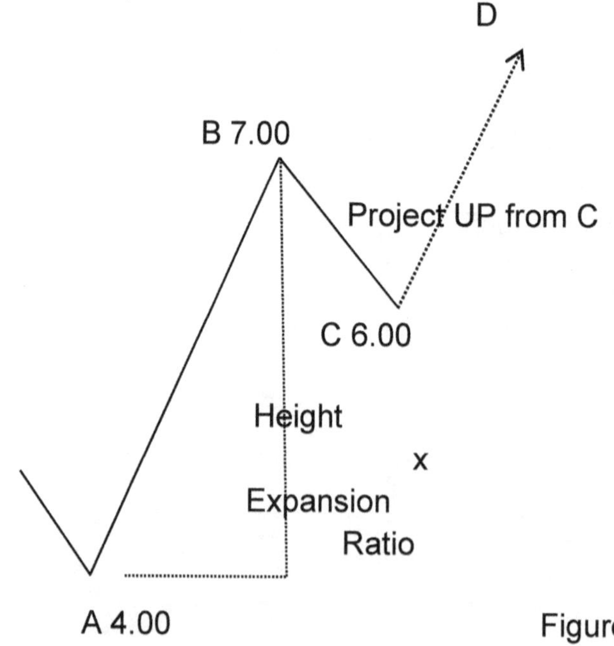

Figure 8

1st Expansion Objective

Height 3.00 x 0.618 = 1.85

Objective: C + 1.85 = 6.00 + 1.85

= 7.85

2nd Expansion Objective

Height 3.00 x 1.0 = 3.00

Objective: C + 3.00 = 6.00 + 3.00

= 9.00

3rd Expansion Objective

Height 3.00 x 1.618 = 4.85

Objective: C + 4.85 = 6.00 + 4.85

= 10.85

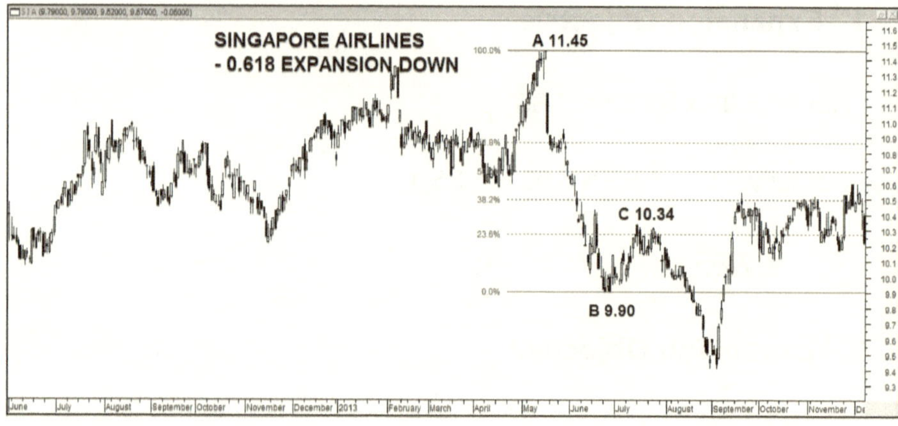

Chart 5.7(a) : 0.618x of height AB

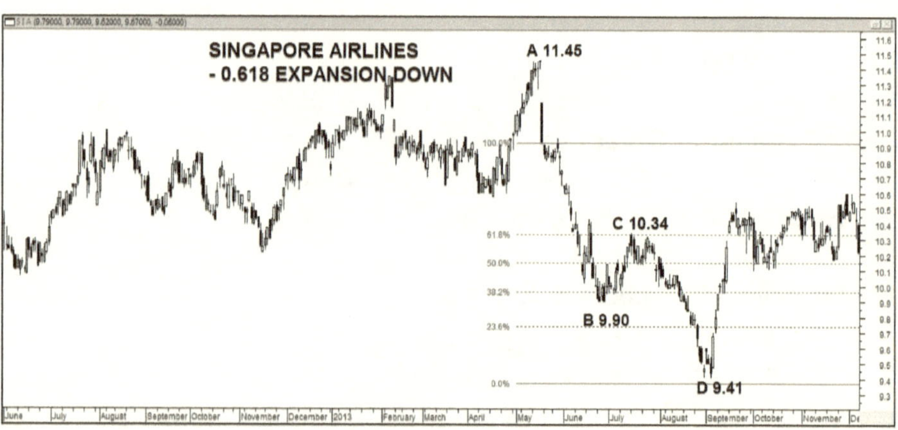

Chart 5.7(b) : 0.618 Expansion DOWN of height AB from Point C to Point D

Chart 5.8(a) : 1.0x of height AB

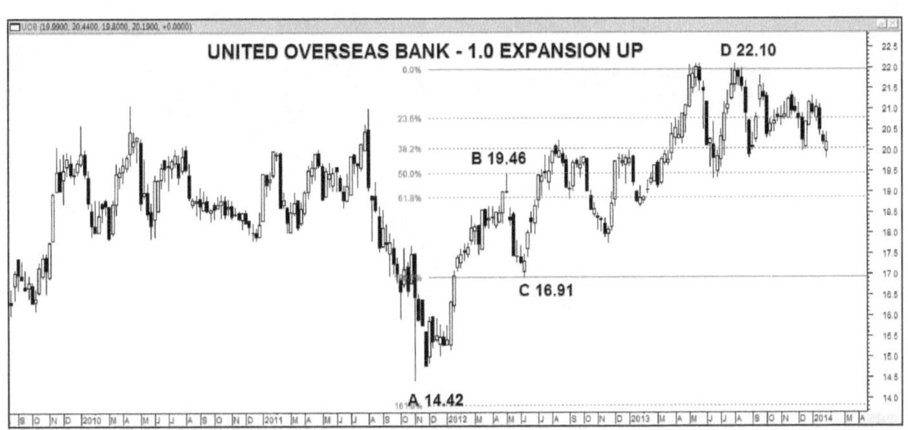

Chart 5.8(b) : 1.0 Expansion UP of height AB from Point C to Point D

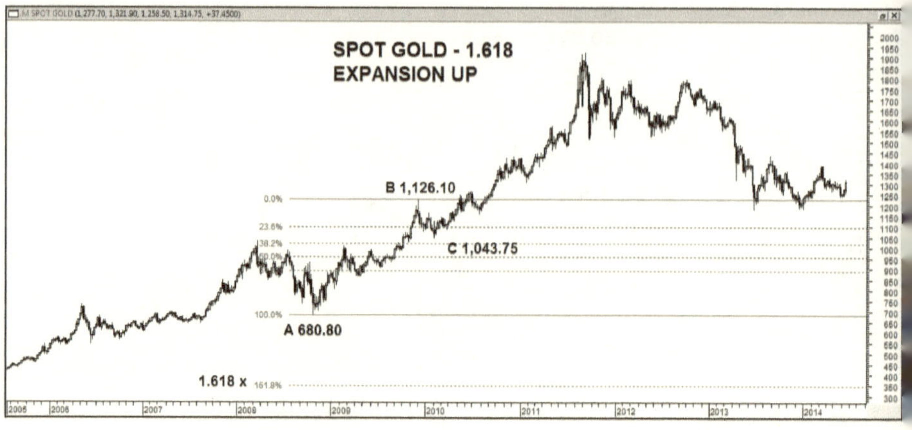

Chart 5.9(a) : 1.618x of height AB

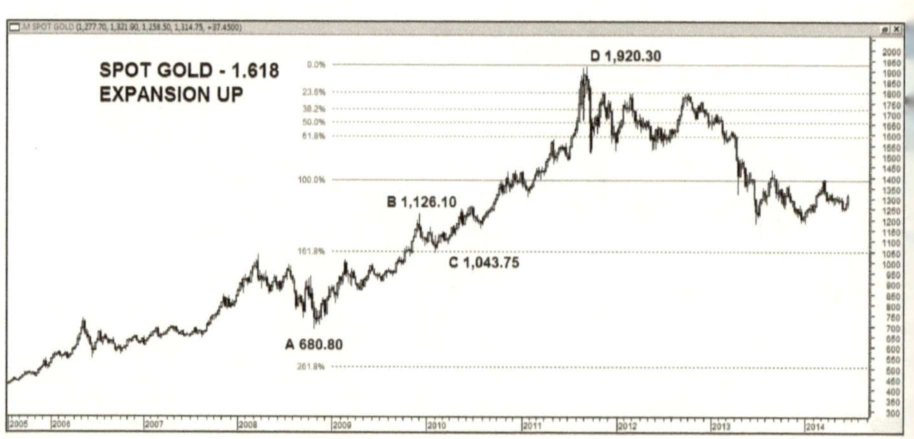

Chart 5.9(b) : 1.618 Expansion UP of height AB from Point C to Point D

Tactical Issues in Fibonacci Technique

(a) The choice of the 2 points of the height is crucial. Start with the <u>major highs and lows</u> in the Daily chart. These can give surprisingly good results – they identify the retracement tops/bottoms.
(b) If the initial points chosen do not produce objectives which work out in the end, experiment with other points. New and more significant highs and lows that emerge subsequently may produce the objectives.

(c) If the Daily chart does not provide the important highs and lows for projection, use the <u>Weekly</u> chart. The Monthly chart may be not be suitable for medium-term objectives.

(d) If we use different ratios and different heights and they end up giving <u>similar objectives</u>, then the objectives arrived at are likely to be significant.

(e) The Fibonacci technique is valuable when markets reach <u>uncharted levels</u>, when previous support/resistance levels are not available as possible objectives.

Conclusion

As stated at the beginning of this chapter, 10/40 EMA and Bollinger Bands are very important indicators to help the investor to arrive at support and resistance levels in the different market scenarios. However, it should be pointed out that moving averages and Bollinger Bands are actually moving targets. They are calculated using the latest closing prices and the levels thus created rise or fall according to the latest prices.

The Fibonacci objective levels however depend on using the selected important highs and lows, and they are independent of the current day-to-day (or even week-to-week) prices. Fibonacci objectives will not shift once the high and low points are selected. If the points selected are important historical levels, the objectives arrived at will not change unless new historical levels are reached. That being the case, the Fibonacci technique does not suffer from the effects of being a moving target. It is thus an important technique to adopt despite the importance of moving averages and Bollinger Bands. And should some of the Fibonacci objective levels coincide with important moving average or Bollinger Band levels, their significance will obviously be increased.

CHAPTER 6 - TIMING WITH STOCHASTICS

The sprinter in timing tools!

Timing is one of the most important and complex issues for investors and traders. Timing involves both entry and exit timing, and timing in trending as well as congesting markets.

The timing indicators that have been proved invaluable are two very old indicators - Stochastics and Moving Average Convergence Divergence (MACD). The main reason I use these two indicators is that both of them have two lines, thus allowing a crossover signal to signal buy and sell timing timings.

It is worth noting that Stochastics and MACD (like people) have different 'personalities' or character because of their different formulation. Stochastics is a relatively faster moving indicator whereas MACD is a slower moving one. That being the case, the way to use the two is to take advantage of their different strengths and use them according to the market environments that suit their 'personalities'. Investors or traders who use only one of these two indicators for all market environments, or for both entry and exit, are likely to encounter problems because that approach ignores their different character and the different market environments.

Stochastics Structure

Y axis range: 0 – 100
Overbought level: 80.
Oversold level: 20

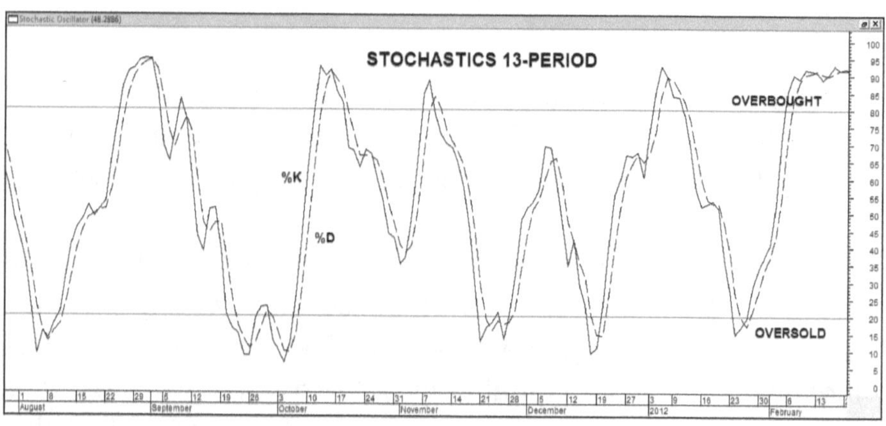

Chart 6.1: Stochastics Structure and Lines, %K & %D

The Stochastics range is between 0 and 100, and the indicator rises and falls in line with price. When price rises to push Stochastics above 80, ie 'Overbought', it suggests that price has risen too much and may turn down. On the other hand, when price falls to push Stochastics to below 20, ie 'Oversold', it suggests that price may have fallen too much and may turn up. However, this is only a general guideline, and may only be valid under certain market conditions. (More scenarios will be explained in this chapter.)

Stochastics Lines
The 2 Stochastics lines are %K and %D, where %K is the dominant line, while %D is a moving average of %K. The default setting for %K is 5 periods, and for %D, it is 3 periods.

Recommendation: <u>13 periods</u> for %K, and 3 periods for %D.
13 periods is preferred for %K because 5 periods is a relatively small number of periods, and tends to produce more signals, which may result in some false signals.

The impact of using 3 periods for %D is that the two lines are close to each other and cross each other easily. With 3-period %D, Stochastics becomes a more sensitive and faster moving timing indicator, which is necessary when one needs a quick reacting timing tool in certain circumstances. Stochastics is balanced by a slower timing tool, which is Moving Average Convergence Divergence (MACD), to be covered in Chapter 7.

Basic buy & sell timing signals
Buy signal: %K crosses ABOVE %D
Sell signal: %K crosses BELOW %D

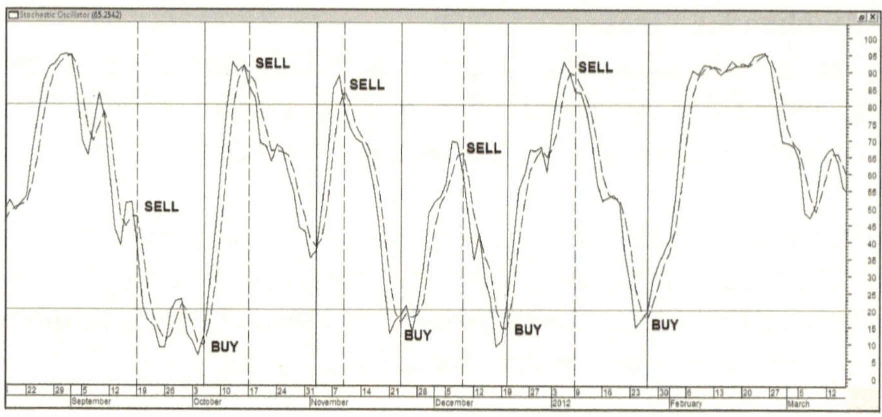

Chart 6.2: Stochastics Basic Buy/Sell Signals

These signals are 'basic' because it is necessary to consider the Stochastics absolute level (eg 20, 50 or 80), when the %K and %D crossover takes place. As Stochastics crossover signals can occur at all levels, it is necessary to have filters to pick the most appropriate signals.

It is also necessary to consider the market trend - congestion or trending.

Stochastics Timing Signals in a Congestion

Stochastics is a valuable timing indicator in that it can be used for BOTH a buy or a sell in a congesting market under the appropriate circumstances.

Within a congestion, price trades to similar highs and lows. Price also tends to turn relatively quickly at the highs and the lows of the range. By formulation, Stochastics is a relatively fast moving indicator, and it moves in tandem with price. When price rises, Stochastics will rise, and when price falls, Stochastics will follow closely. Within a congestion, Stochastics tends to top off when price reaches its upper limit, i.e. above 80, and price tends to bottom out when Stochastics reaches below 20.

Buy & Sell Timing

A good Stochastics buy signal occurs when Stochastics is below 20, and turns up. The precise timing to buy is when %K line crosses above %D line when both lines are both below 20. It should be pointed out that Stochastics being below 20 alone is NOT a buy signal; the %K-%D cross-up is the signal.

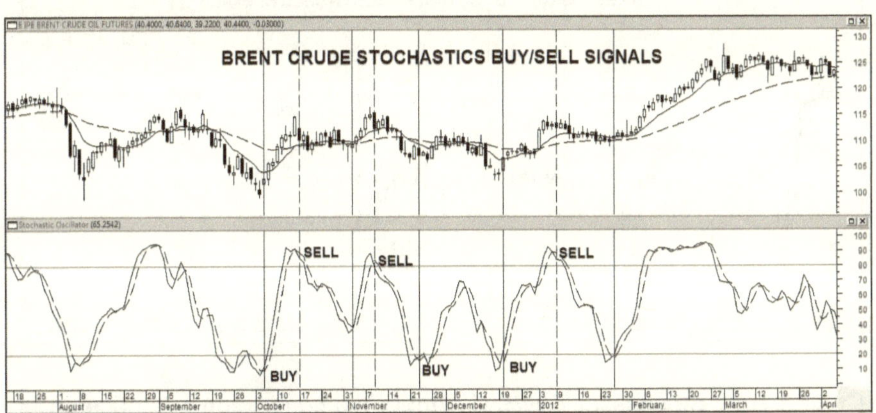

Chart 6.3(a): Stochastics Buy/Sell Signals in a Congestion

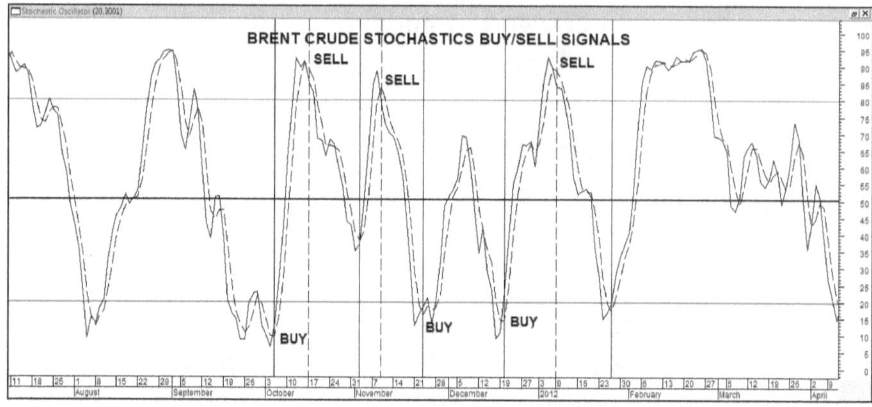

Chart 6.3(b) : Stochastics Buy/Sell signals

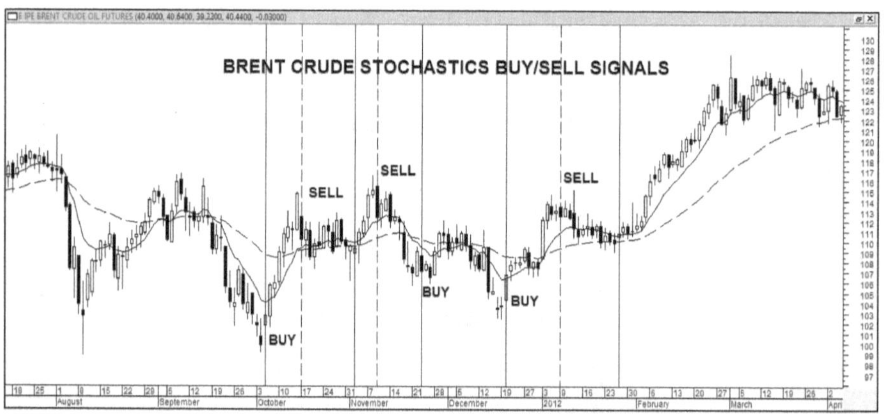

Chart 6.3(c) : Stochastics Buy/Sell signals in a congestion with price action

In the same way, a good sell signal in congestion occurs when Stochastics is <u>above 80</u> and turns down. The precise sell timing is when %K crosses <u>below</u> %D when both lines are above 80.

<u>Important</u> : When the above sell signal occurs, the price is likely to be declining from the highest bar of the congestion.

Similarly, when the buy signal occurs, the price is likely to be rising after the lowest bar of the congestion. This is because the %K-%D crossover occurs only <u>after</u> the price bar has either fallen from the highest point, or risen from the lowest point. But suffice to say, it is a good enough signal to buy or sell at the second bar from the top or bottom!

As price trades in the middle of a congestion, Stochastics buy and sell signals will occur in between 20 and 80 as price fluctuates. Such Stochastics buy and sell signals should be ignored simply because one would be buying or selling in the middle of the congestion, and not at the highs and lows of the congestion which are obviously the preferred entry levels.

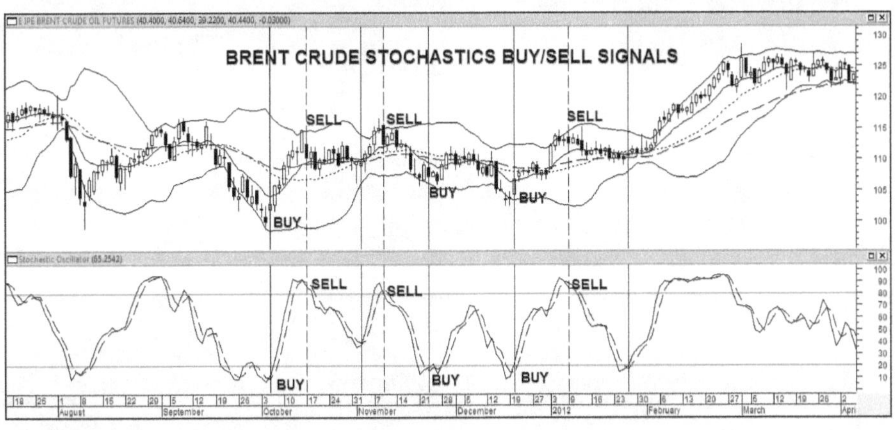

Chart 6.4: Stochastics Buy/Sell Signals in a Congestion with Bollinger Bands

Other Indicators: See Chapter 8 on Integrating Trend, Timing & Price for Integrating Bollinger Bands with Stochastics in a congestion.

Stochastics Buy Timing in an Uptrend

Stochastics is ideal for timing a buy entry during the retracement move of an uptrend. As long as price is trending, Stochastics tends to be in the overbought region, i.e. above 80 levels.

When price retraces down past the 10 EMA, Stochastics will fall BELOW 50 level. As the correction ends and the uptrend resumes, the rising price triggers %K to cross above %D, and creates a valid buy signal. This buy signal occurring from the 50 level is one of the powerful signals from Stochastics, and is worth waiting for.

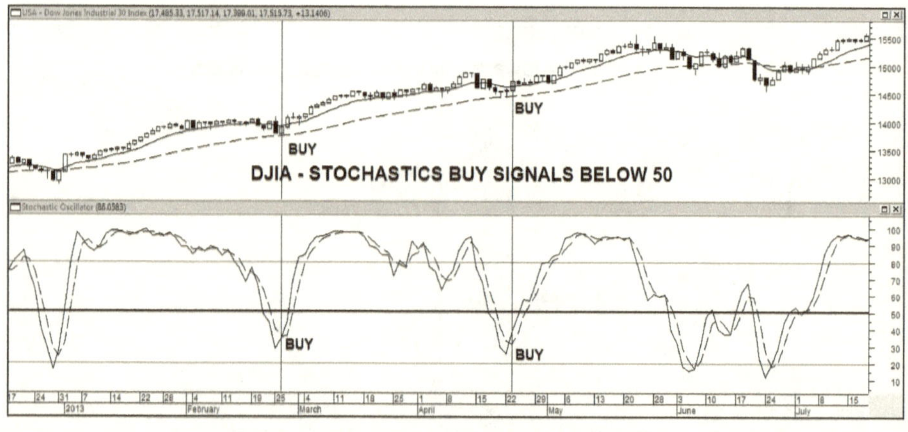

Chart 6.5(a) : Stochastics Buy signals in an uptrend for DJIA

If the correction is deeper, the falling price may pull Stochastics all the way down to the 20 level. And when price resumes up, it will trigger %K to cross above %D, leading to a buy signal as well.

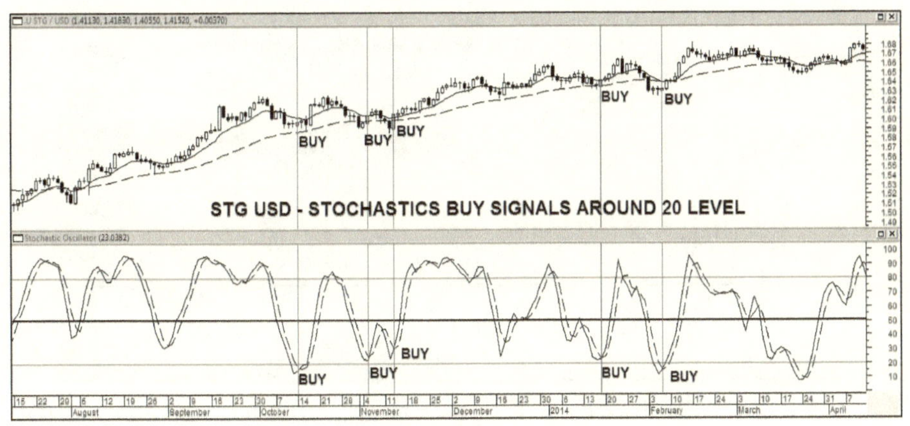

Chart 6.5(b) : Stochastics Buy signals in an uptrend for STG USD

Stochastics Sell Timing in a Downtrend

In a downtrend, Stochastics will produce a valid sell signal at the end of a retracement up. In the retracement up, Stochastics recovers ABOVE the 50 level. When price resumes down, it will trigger a sell signal, with %K crossing below %D. This is a powerful sell signal from Stochastics in the downtrend.

Again as in the uptrend, when the retracement up is stronger, Stochastics will trade to the 80 level. And when price turns down, %K crosses below %D, triggering a very good sell signal.

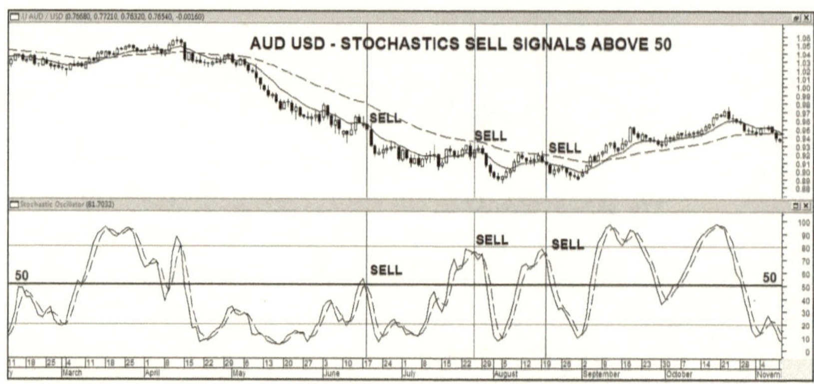

Chart 6.6(a) : Stochastics Sell signals above 50 in a downtrend for AUD USD

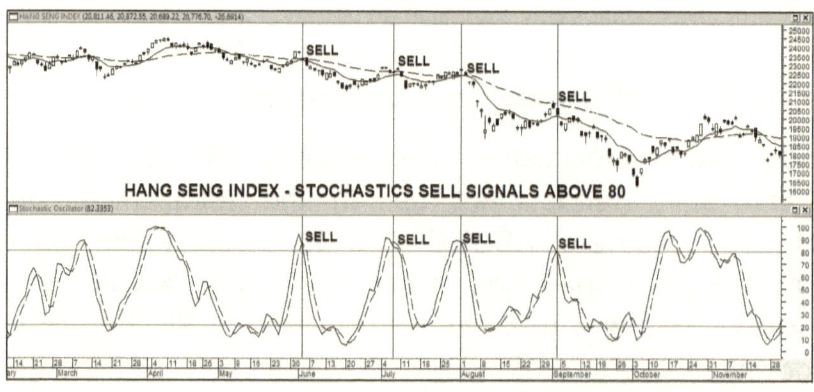

Chart 6.6(b) : Stochastics Sell signals above 80 in a downtrend for Hang Seng Index

Why do Stochastics timing signals work in trends?

It should be pointed out that Stochastics works well in the above scenarios because it is a quick acting timing indicator. This is because of the formulation of %D as a small (3-period) moving average of %K. This means that the two lines will cross when a small turn in price takes place. Should a larger %D value be used, the crossover signal will be slower and it will end up producing later signals which are not ideal when a quick signal is needed at the end of retracement.

Stochastics Counter-trend Signals in a Trending Market

In a strong trending market, price is either continuously rising or falling. In an uptrend, Stochastics is driven by the rising prices to remain above 80 level. At that level, many sell signals will be triggered by small moves down, but these sell signals do not typically produce deep corrections down. These sell signals <u>should not be followed</u>, unlike in a congestion.

Similarly, in a downtrend, Stochastics is driven by falling prices to remain below 20 level. As in the uptrend, many buy signals will be triggered by minor moves up, but these buy signals may not produce price rises, and should not be followed.

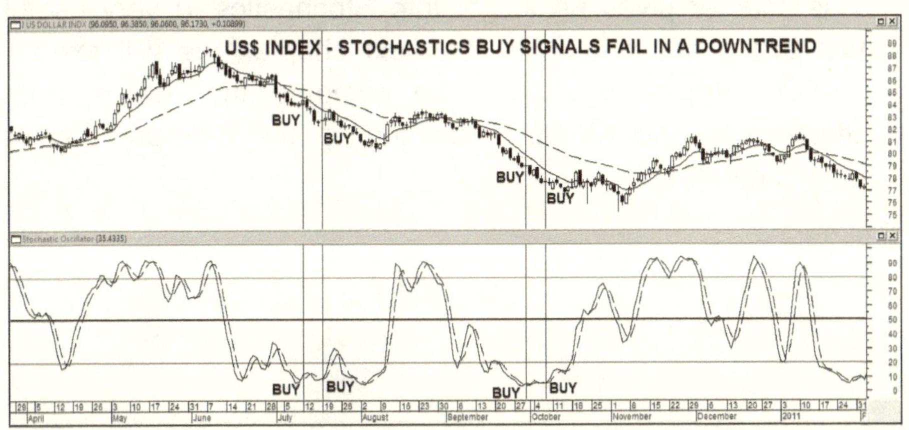

Chart 6.7(a) : Stochastics Buy signals fail in a downtrend for USD Index

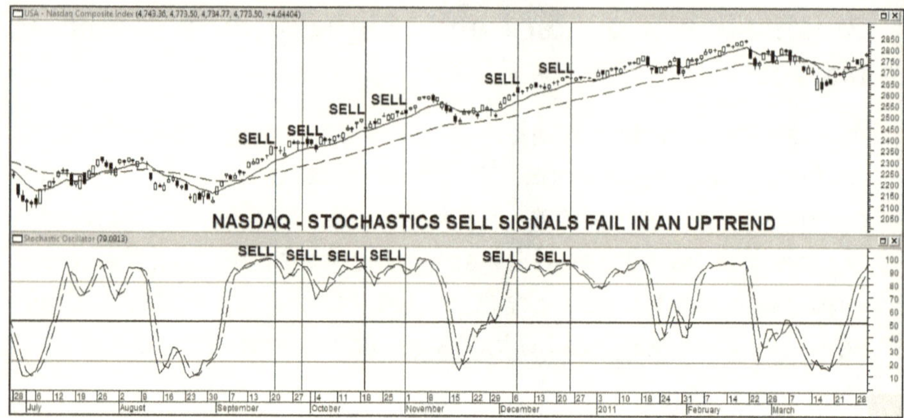

Chart 6.7(b) : Stochastics sell signals fail in an uptrend for NASDAQ

Conclusion

This chapter gives an insght into Stochastics, a very useful fast acting timing tool. In the next chapter, we will explain MACD's applications and also compare the use of both Stochastics and MACD according to the different market environments.

CHAPTER 7 - TIMING WITH MOVING AVERAGE CONVERGENCE DIVERGENCE (MACD)

Slow & steady, the marathoner in timing tools.

Moving Average Convergence Divergence (MACD) is the second and a very valuable timing tool in your tool box as it complements Stochastics. MACD is a slower moving timing indicator because of its formulation; it has an important role when an investor needs an indicator to keep a position longer in the market instead of getting it sooner.

MACD Formulation

MACD consists of 2 lines, the MACD line itself, and the Signal Line -
MACD's default formulation: the difference between the 12 and 26 EMA of closing price.
Signal Line (SL): 9-period EMA of MACD itself.
Y axis: These two lines oscillate around the Equilibrium or zero line.

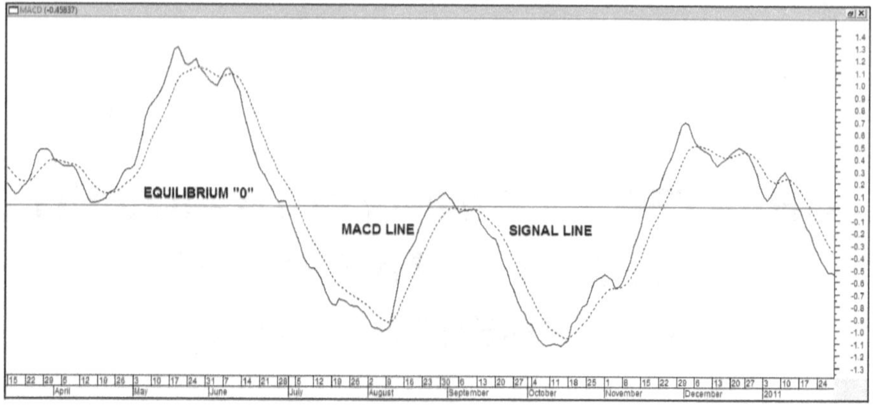

Chart 7.1: MACD structure and lines

MACD offers 3 signals to the investor – trend signal, divergence signal and timing signal. While its timing signal is possibly its most important signal, the other two are worth knowing well.

MACD Trend Signal

MACD signals that a market is Uptrend when MACD line (not SL) is above the Equilibrium or zero line.

MACD signals that a market is Downtrend when MACD line (not SL) is below the Equilibrium or zero line.

The point of change is when the MACD line crosses the Equilibrium or zero line.

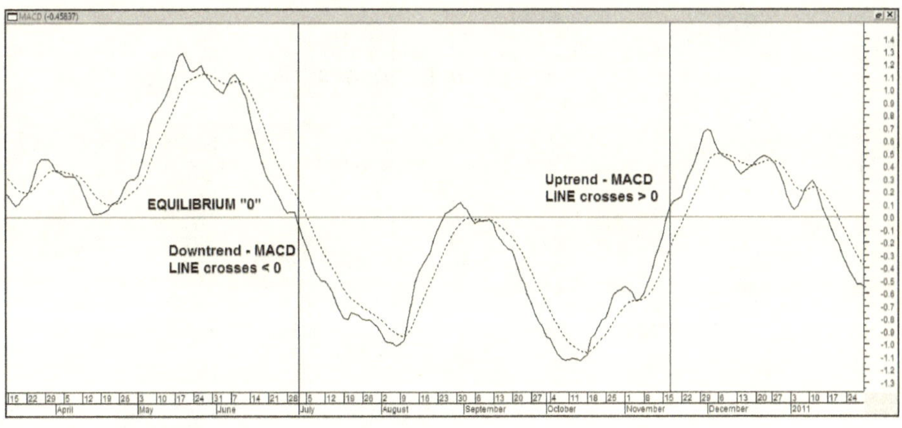

Chart 7.2(a): MACD trend signals

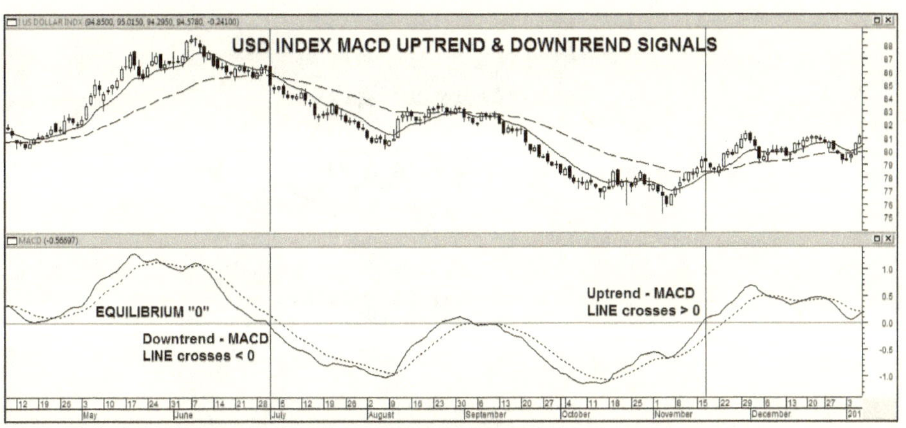

Chart 7.2(b): MACD Uptrend & Downtrend Signals

When a market is in a Congestion, MACD crosses and re-crosses the Equilibrium line repeatedly, as long as price remains sideway.

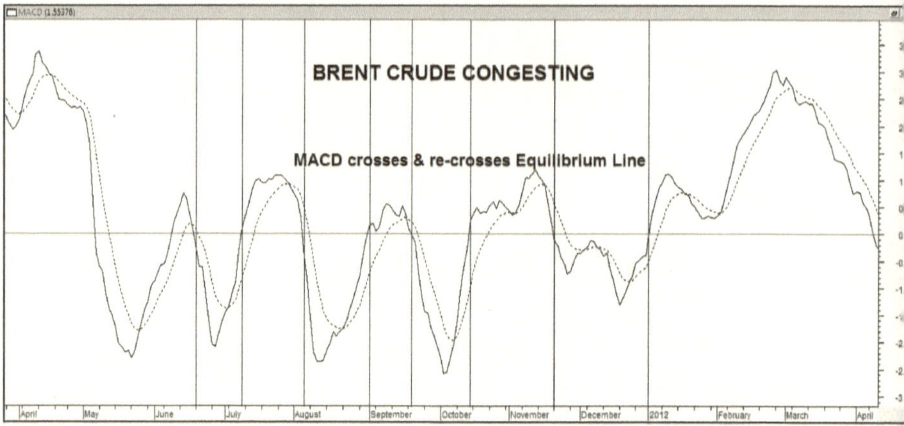

Chart 7.3(a): MACD congestion signal – MACD crosses and recrosses Equilibrium line

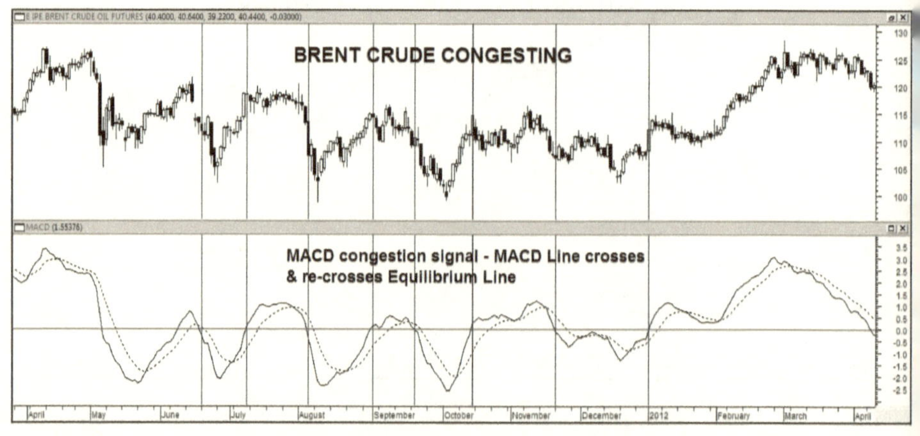

Chart 7.3(b): MACD Congestion Signal confirmed by price

Comparing MACD Trend Signal with 10/40 EMA

Broadly, MACD's trend signal is similar to the 10/40 EMA crossover signal as the MACD is the calculated using the 12 EMA and 26 EMA which is not a big difference mathematically from 10/40 EMA. It should be noted that the MACD trend signal occurs <u>earlier</u> than the 10/40 crossover in the same move as it uses smaller MA's, 12 and 26. Hence it can be used as an advanced signal to the 10/40 crossover.

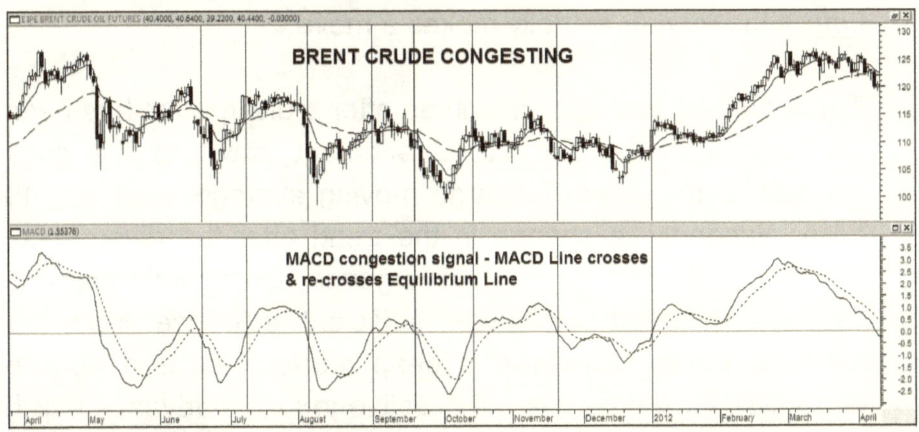

Chart 7.4: Comparing MACD congestion signals with 10/40 EMA signals

MACD Divergence Signal

Definition of Divergence

Divergence happens when the market price and an accompanying technical indicator are in a divergent condition. It occurs in a trending market, both uptrend and downtrend, but not in a congestion.

Uptrend Divergence: In an uptrend, price reaches a <u>higher high</u>, but the indicator only reaches a <u>lower high</u> at the second of the two corresponding points.

<u>Downtrend</u> Divergence: In a downtrend, price reaches a <u>lower low</u>, but MACD already reaches a <u>higher low</u> at the second of the two corresponding points.

Impact of Divergence Signal

The divergence signal is extremely useful in that it is an <u>advance</u> technical signal. When Divergence happens, it tells the investor of a potential change in market sentiments even <u>before</u> the market actually makes a move.

There are two possible outcomes after a divergence has been identified – firstly, a deep retracement in which the price corrects to the level of a large moving average level, eg, 40 EMA. Secondly, a change in the trend after the divergence. Some practitioners say that divergence consistently leads to changes in trend. However, sufficient evidence from the markets proves otherwise; a deep retracement is a definite possibility. However, it is not possible to say in advance which outcome, retracement or change in trend, will follow.

The following charts show the two possible results of a Divergence signal, in uptrend and downtrend situations.

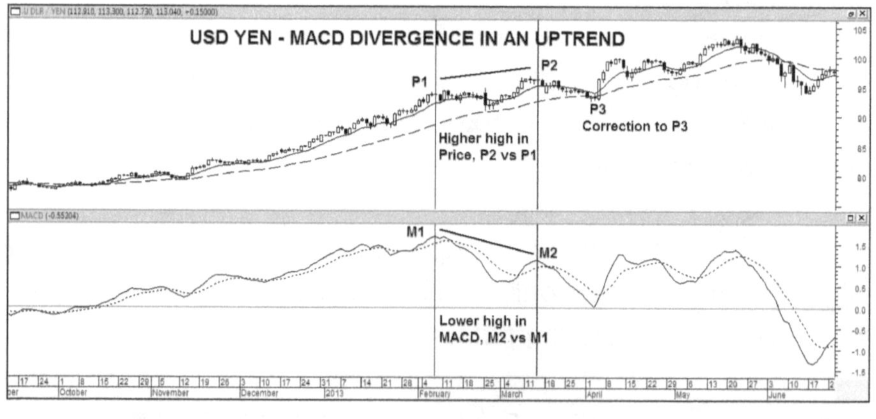

Chart 7.5: MACD Divergence Signal in an uptrend leading to a correction

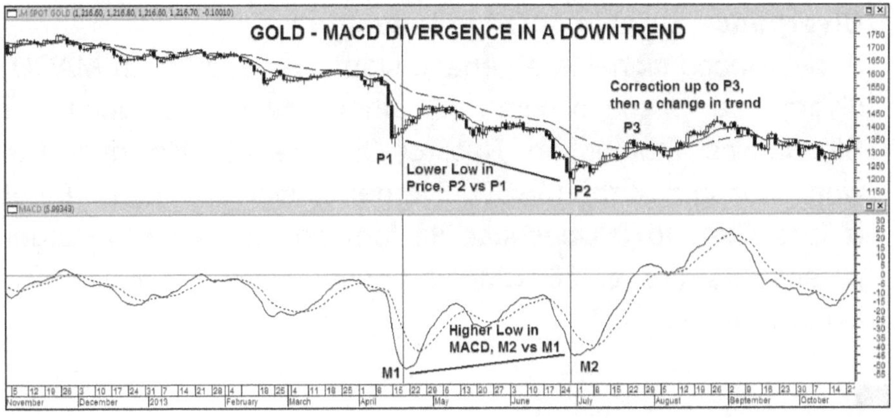

Chart 7.6: MACD Divergence Signal in a downtrend leading to a change to uptrend.

Timing of Divergence Signal

Divergence does not happen early in a trend. In the early part of an uptrend, price and MACD tend to be convergent, that is to say, higher high in price is matched by corresponding higher high in MACD. This can continue for a considerable part of the trend before a divergence occurs, whether uptrend or downtrend. So investors should not look for divergence to occur early in a trend. The same is true in a downtrend.

Is a change of trend always preceded by divergence?

Not so. Trend change often occurs without a divergence. If divergence happens, it is a bonus signal for the investor. In any case, as stated earlier, divergence does lead only to a correction and not a change in trend.

Divergence Signals of Other Indicators

A divergence signal is a generic signal; so apart from MACD, divergence also occurs in other oscillators such as Stochastics, Momentum, Rate of Change, etc. However it is worth noting that the MACD divergence signal is the one that is less likely to fail because its formulation based on larger parameters (12 & 26 EMA of price) removes divergence signals that may fail.

MACD Timing Signals

The MACD timing signals are its most important signal, not least because there are few two-lined indicators apart from MACD and Stochastics.

Buy timing: When MACD crosses ABOVE Signal Line.
Sell timing: When MACD crosses BELOW Signal Line.

The implication of the basic MACD buy and sell signals is that price is likely to rise or fall after the signals occur.

Both MACD buy and sell signals are slow, it takes several periods of price movement to trigger a buy or sell signal. The first reason is the MACD itself is based on 12 and 26 EMA of price, which are relatively large numbers. Because of the large numbers, the MACD line does not react quickly to price fluctuations.

Secondly, the SL, a 9-period MA of the MACD value, is a relatively large value for a crossover line (compared to 3-period %D for Stochastics). The gap between MACD and the

SL is relatively wide. As a result a larger price move is needed before a MACD-SL cross-over can happen.

The outcome is that MACD is a slow timing tool. This 'slowness' can be viewed by some as a disadvantage, but it can also be an advantage depending how MACD is used and the environment it is used in.

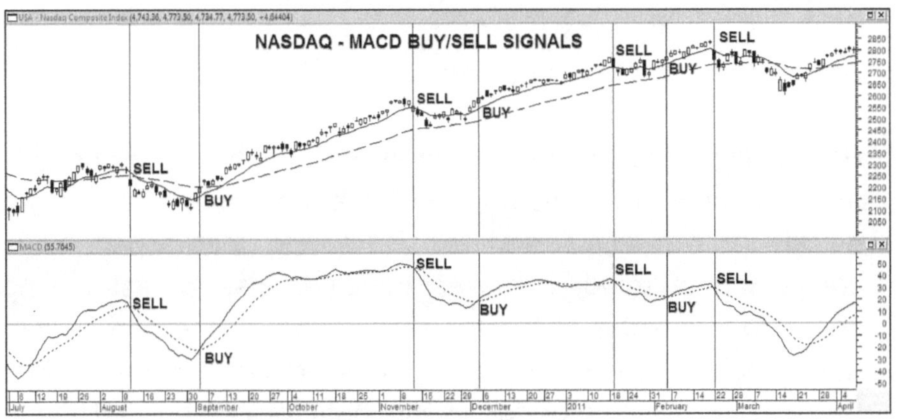

Chart 7.7: MACD Buy & Sell Signals

MACD & Stochastics Compared

Differences in Formulation

The recommendation for Stochastics formulation is 13 periods for %K, and 3 periods for %D. Using a 3-period %D, the crossover signal between %K and %D is triggered easily. With the 13-3 formulation, Stochastics is a faster and more responsive timing indicator compared to MACD.

The question which arises for investors is, which is the better timing tool? The answer is not which is the better indicator, but which one meets the needs of the investor in the different market environments.

In essence, both MACD and Stochastics are needed by the investor, because investors can take advantage of their difference, fast and slow timing tools, to meet the investor's needs in different market environments – to enter or exit, in congesting or trending markets.

Stochastics or MACD in Congestions?

Prices within a congestion trade in a range. While the price is more often in the mid-range of the congestion, they turn quickly at the highs and lows. Bearing this aspect of a congestion in mind, it makes sense to use a fast-moving timing tool to enter at the top and bottom of the congestion, rather than a slow-moving timing tool. Stochastics is therefore the preferred indicator for timing both buys and sells in a congestion. The %K - %D crossover signals typically occur 1-2 bars from the highs or lows.

What if the investor uses MACD? The indicator's 'slower' reaction means that the buy/sell signals will only be triggered several bars after the lows/highs of the congestion. In fact by the time the MACD crosses the SL to produce a buy or sell timing, the market is typically in the mid-range of the congestion, which is not a preferred buy/sell level.

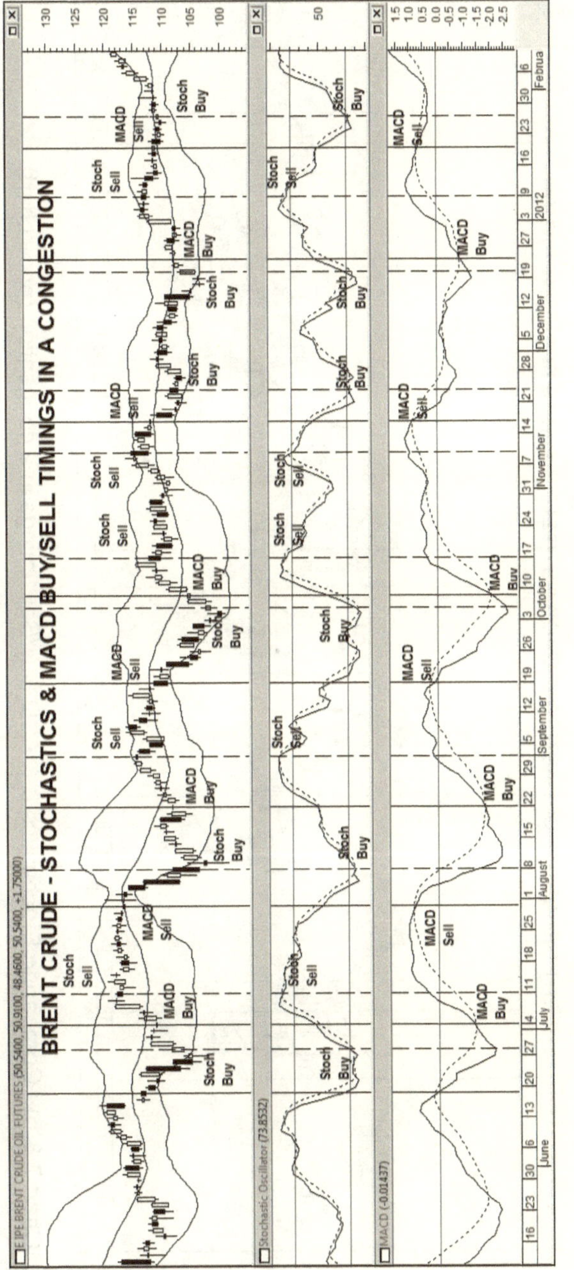

Chart 7.8(a): Comparing MACD & Stochastics Buy/Sell timings in a congestion

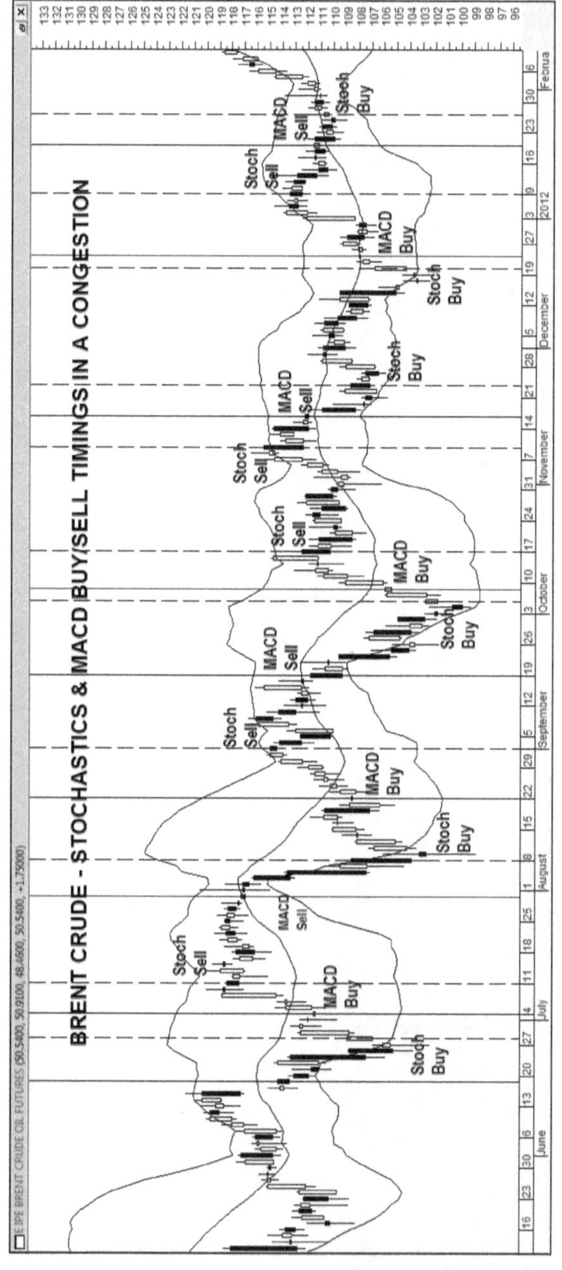

Chart 7.8(b) : Comparing Stochastics & MACD Buy/Sell timings in a congestion (price chart)

Stochastics or MACD Entry Signal in Trending Markets?

In a trending market, the trending phase is longer than the retracement phase. After a correction however, price turns up relatively quickly back into the trending phase.

The investor should therefore deploy the appropriate timing tool to fit this scenario. Stochastics, the faster and more responsive timing indicator can be used for entry to buy in the resumption of the uptrend, or for entry to sell in the resumption of the downtrend.

What if the investor uses MACD instead? The 'slower' reaction of MACD means that the buy signal will only be triggered several bars after the resumption of the dominant trend. In an uptrend, the MACD will trigger a high buy, whereas in a downtrend, it will trigger a low sell, both of which will be less favourable compared to Stochastics for the investor.

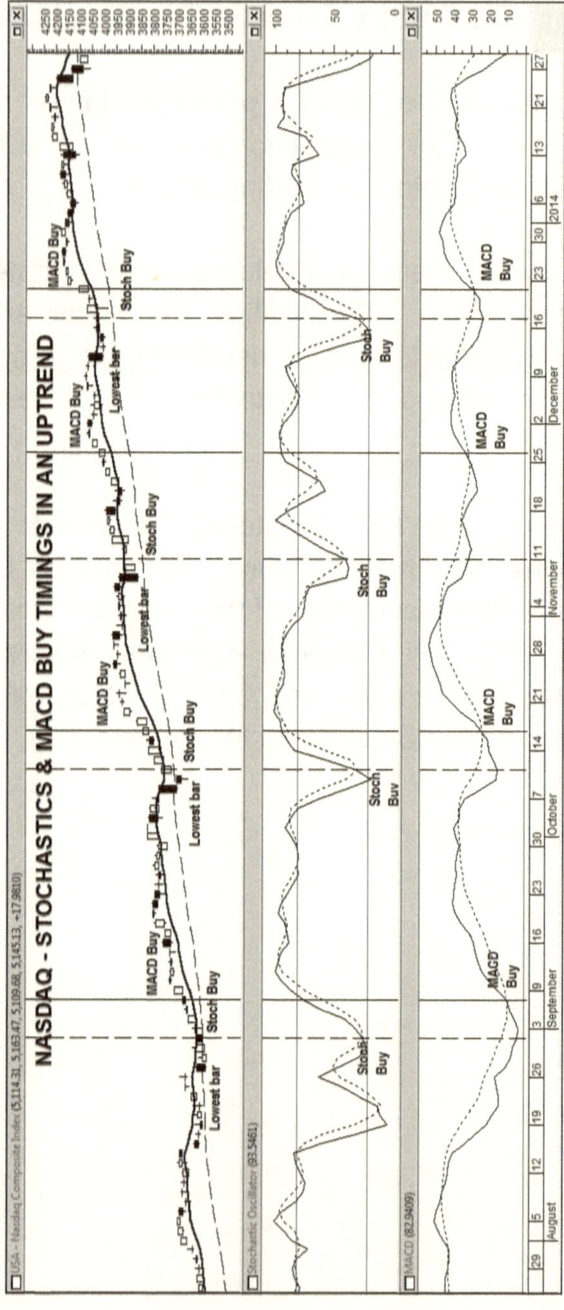

Chart 7.9(a) : Comparing Stochastics & MACD Buy Timings in an uptrend

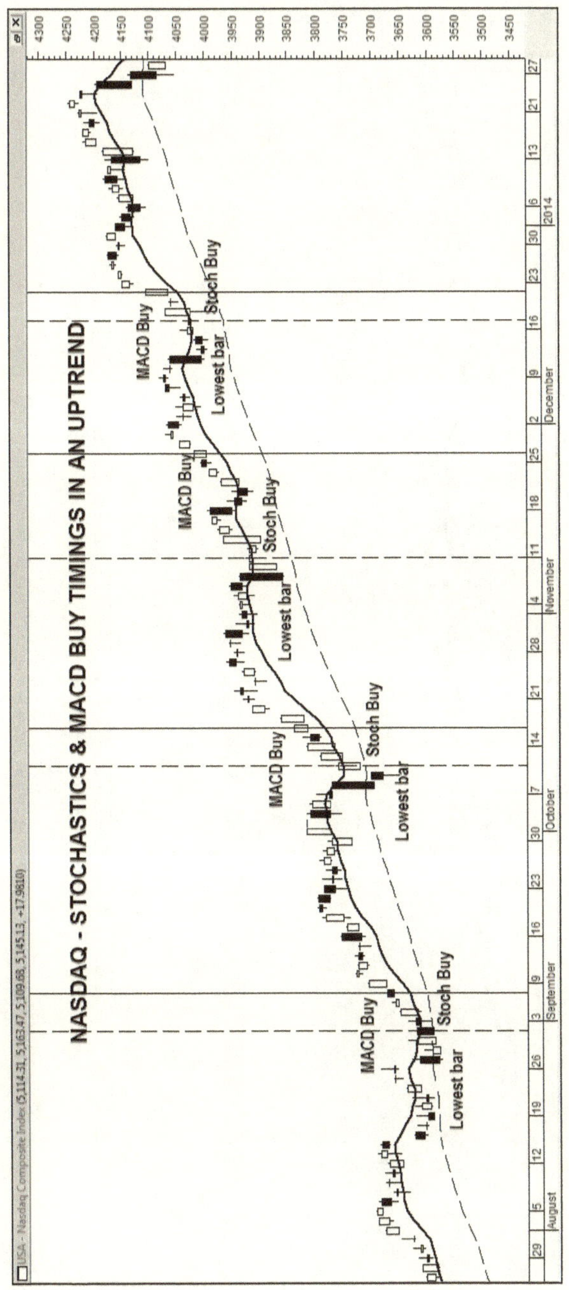

Chart 7.9(b) : Comparing Stochastics & MACD Buy Timings in an uptrend (price chart)

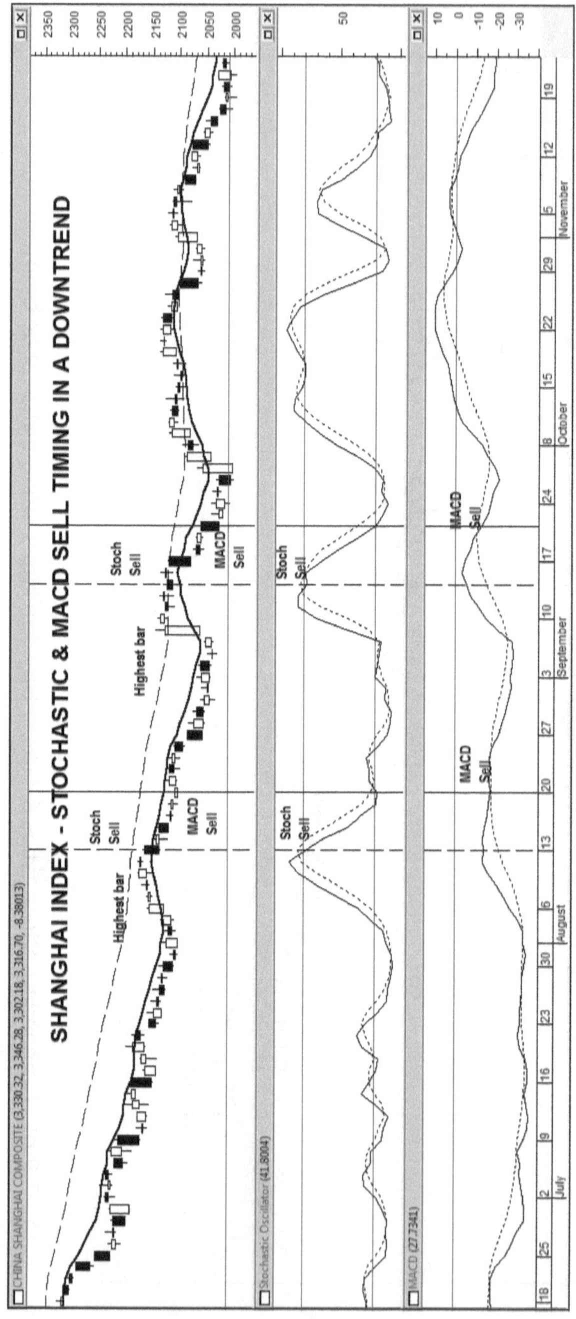

Chart 7.10(a) : Comparing Stochastics & MACD Sell Timings in a downtrend

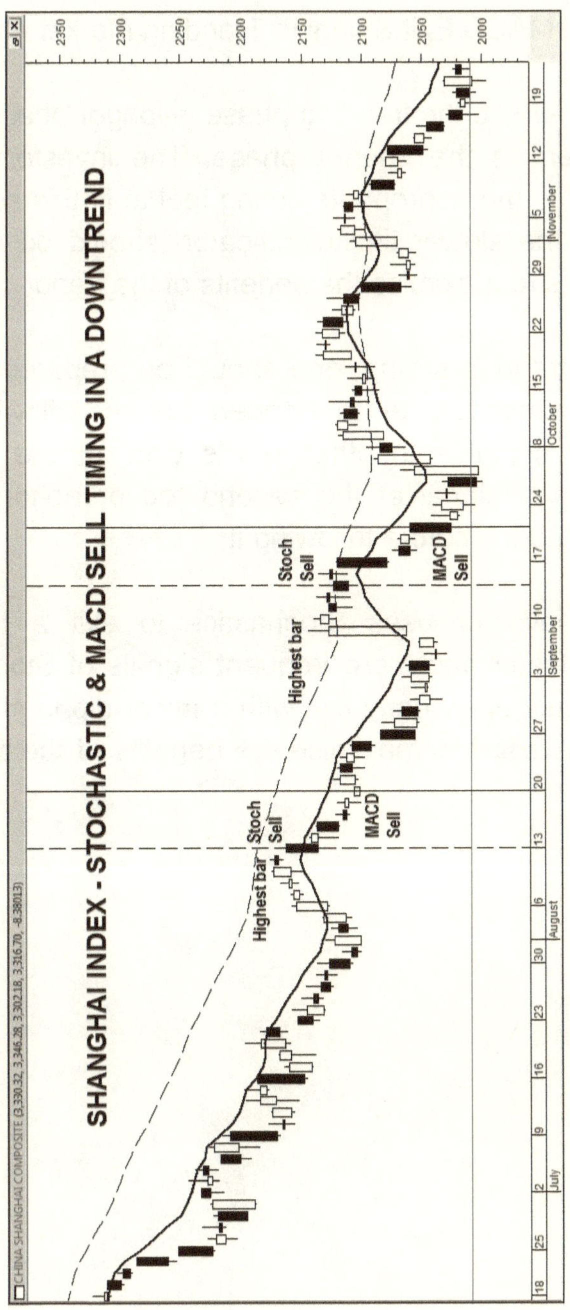

Chart 7.10(b) : Comparing Stochastics & MACD Sell Timings in a downtrend (Price chart)

Stochastics or MACD Exit Signal in Trending Markets?

In a trending market, the trending phase is longer phase, while the retracement is the shorter phase. The investor should therefore deploy the appropriate timing tool to fit this scenario. MACD being the slower timing indicator, should be used to time exits so as to maximise the benefits of the trend.

In fact, if the trend is strong, one should be prepared to wait for the divergence signal to happen before following the MACD timing signal – in other words wait for the second MACD crossover signal at the second top or bottom when divergence happens before following it.

What if the investor uses Stochastics to exit a trending market? The faster and more frequent signals of Stochastics will definitely trigger an early exit with a minor dip in price and not help the investor to maximise the benefits of the trending market.

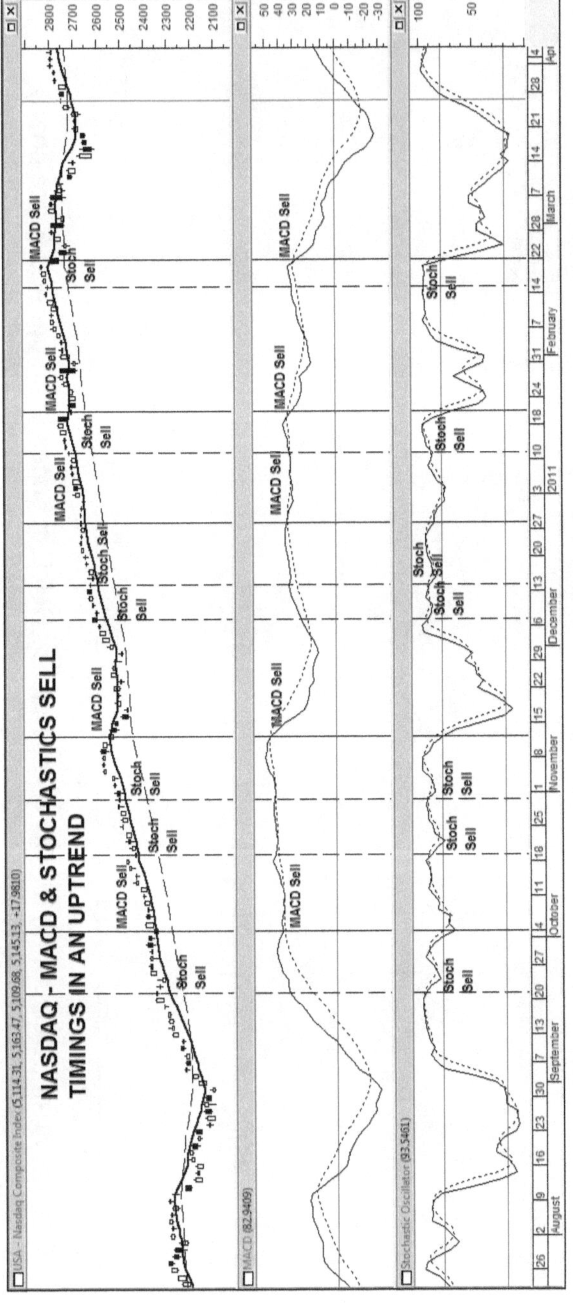

Chart 7.11(a) : Comparing MACD & Stochastics Sell Exit in an uptrend

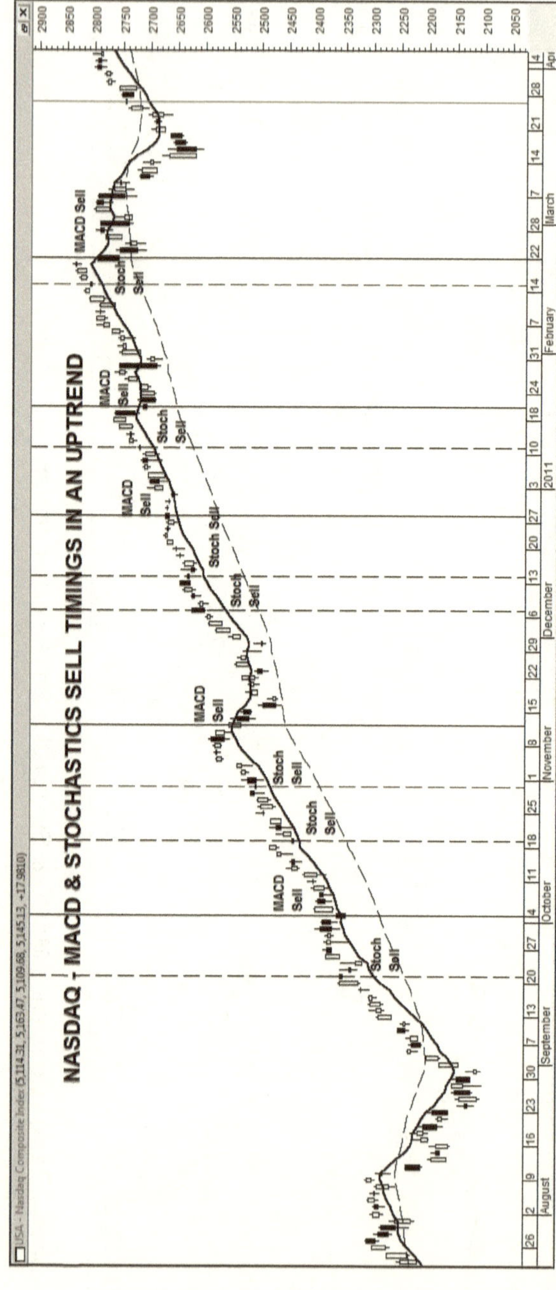

Chart 7.11(b) : Comparing MACD & Stochastics Sell Exit prices in an uptrend (price chart)

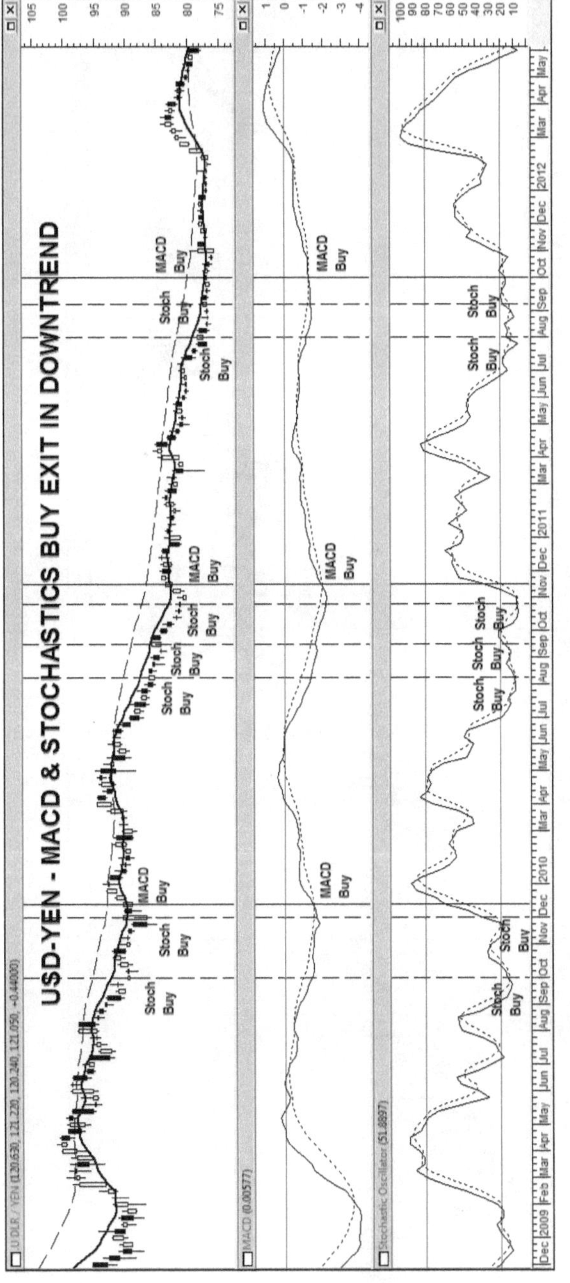

Chart 7.12(a) : Comparing MACD & Stochastics Buy Exit in a downtrend

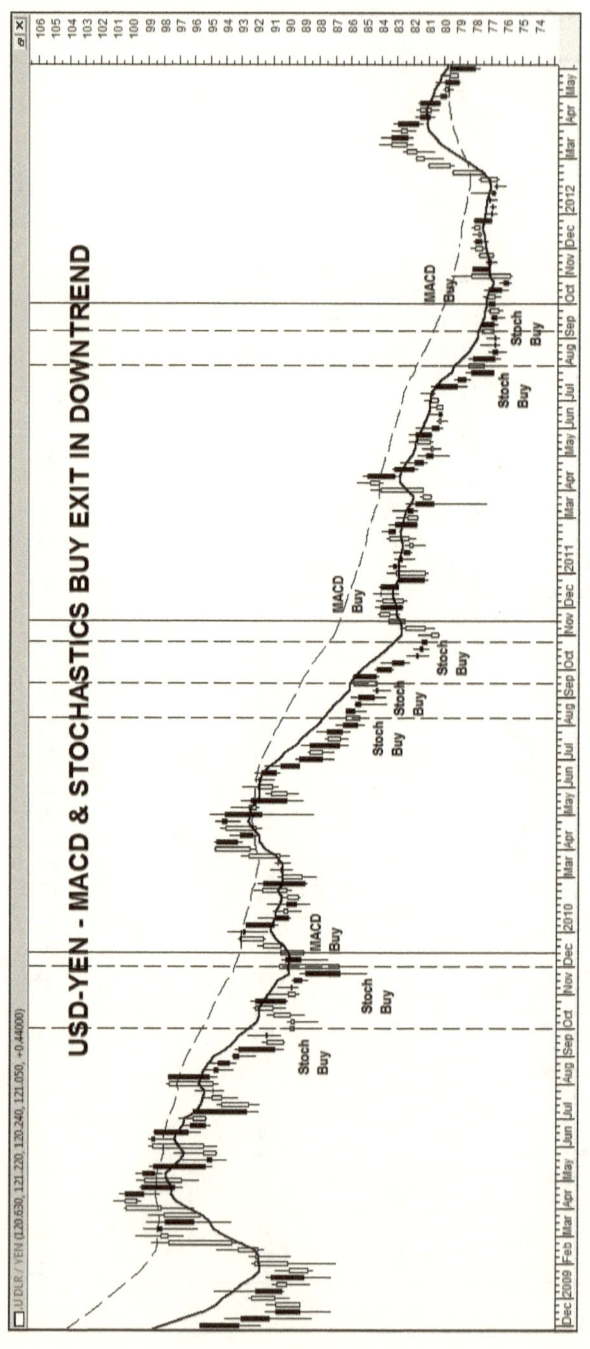

Chart 7.12(b) : Comparing MACD & Stochastics Buy Exit prices in a downtrend (price chart)

Conclusion

Stochastics and MACD are time tested indicators with different "personalities". It is hoped that the two chapters here have helped investors understand these two classic indicators better to decide on their use for timing entry and exit in both congestions and the trending market. Over the years, my understanding of these two indicators has deepened to my advantage.

CHAPTER 8 - INTEGRATING TREND, PRICE & TIMING

Integration is the key!

The basic principle of investment and trading is trading with the trend. If a market is on an uptrend, trading with the trend means buy on dips; and in a downtrend, it will be selling on rallies. Integrating trend with price and timing means that based on a market's trend, technical indicators should provide a 'right' price and a 'right' timing to enter and exit the market. This chapter is devoted to integrating these signals.

Summary of 10/40 EMA Signals

In chapter 3, trend was defined by the 10/40 EMA as follows -

Trend
Uptrend: 10 EMA > 40 EMA
Downtrend: 10 EMA < 40 EMA
Congestion: 10 EMA criss-crosses 40 EMA.

10 and 40 EMA's play the roles of support and resistance as follows -
Uptrend: 10 EMA first support; 40 EMA second support.
Downtrend: 10 EMA first resistance, 40 EMA second resistance.

Congestion: 10 EMA & 40 EMA have no support/resistance roles. Price cuts through both EMA's.

It is worth reiterating that these signals are good for all time frames, Daily, Weekly, Monthly and so on.

Summary of Stochastics Signals

In Chapter 6 it was shown that Stochastics produces good timing signals in line with the trend. In an uptrend (when 10 EMA>40 EMA), if the trend is strong, Stochastics often stays above level 80, falling only a little and still staying above 80 when minor corrections take place.

In a deeper correction down, Stochastics will fall BELOW 50, but when price resumes up, %K crosses back ABOVE %D triggering a buy signal.

In a downtrend (10 EMA<40 EMA), if price is weak, Stochastics often stays below level 20, rising only a little when minor corrections take place. In a stronger correction up, Stochastics will rise ABOVE 50, but when price resumes down, %K crosses back BELOW %D triggering a sell signal.

In congestion (10 EMA criss-crosses 40 EMA) however, because there is an even chance of price moving up and down within a range, Stochastics normally fluctuates between levels 80 and 20, and not staying at either extremes like when the market is trending. When Stochastics is above 80 it signals the upper end of the congestion, and when Stochastics is below 20, price tends to be at the lower end of the congestion.

Sell signal: When %K crosses below %D above 80.
Buy signal: When %K crosses above %D below 20.

Do not follow: Buy or sell signals between 80 and 20, as price is likely to be in the middle of the congestion, and are not the best entry levels.

Summary of Bollinger Band Signals

In Chapter 4, it was stated that when price trades outside of the Band, it retraces back in as a Flag. Support/resistance in the flag tends to be at 10 EMA.

Support & resistance in a Congestion
Upper Band is the resistance
Lower Band is the support.

Any penetration outside of these two bands tend to be short-lived, as price re-enters the Band. However there will be occasions when price does fail to reach the Upper and Lower Bands in a congestion.

INTEGRATION

CHANGE OF TREND

1. Integrating 10/40 EMA Change of trend with Price Action

At the 10/40 crossover signal for change of trend, the most visible and often accurate signal in price action which reinforces the 10/40 signal are the <u>breakaway gaps and long bars</u>. These two price signals provide important confirmation. Additionally, one can also bear in mind that in the case of breakaway gaps at this point, the gap may not be filled.

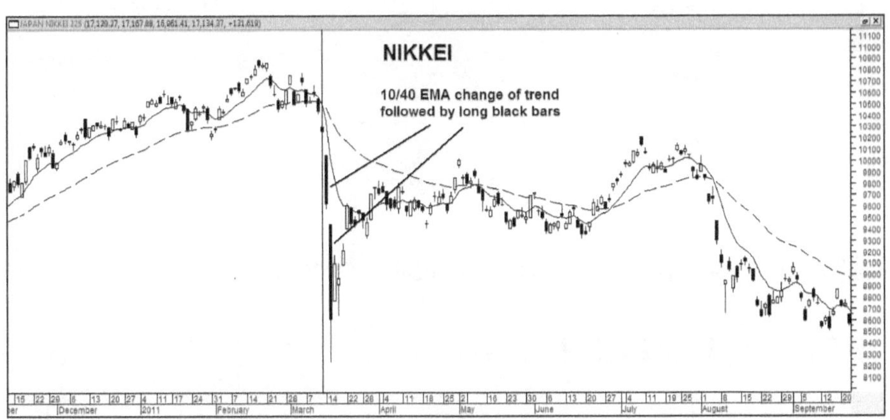

Chart 8.1: Integrating 10/40 EMA change of trend with price action

2. Integrating 10/40 EMA Change of trend with MACD

At the 10/40 crossover signal for change of trend, monitor MACD's crossing its Equilibrium line, which provides the early or simultaneous signal for change in trend.

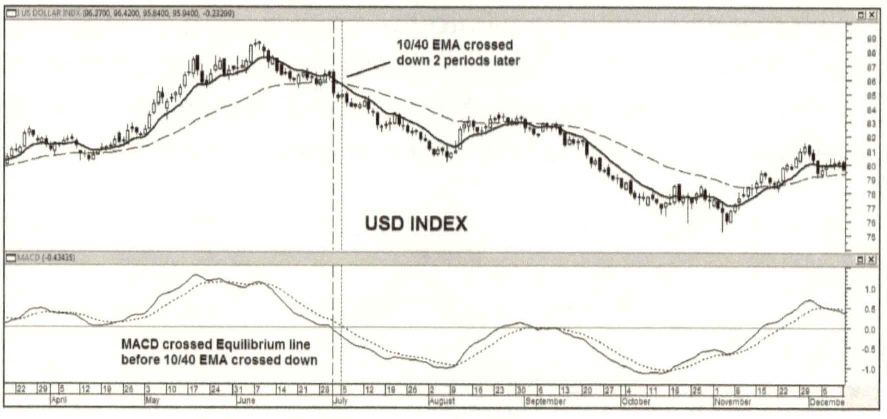

Chart 8.2: Integrating 10/40 EMA change of trend with MACD

RESUMPTION OF TREND

3. Integrating 10/40 EMA with various indicators in Resumption of trend

In a deep retracement, price retraces beyond 10 EMA to reach 40 EMA.

Downtrend

(a) A sizeable retracement up typically ends at the 40 EMA resistance. When price resumes downtrend, the important signal is when price trades back below the 10 EMA. This often signals the continuation of the previous trend.

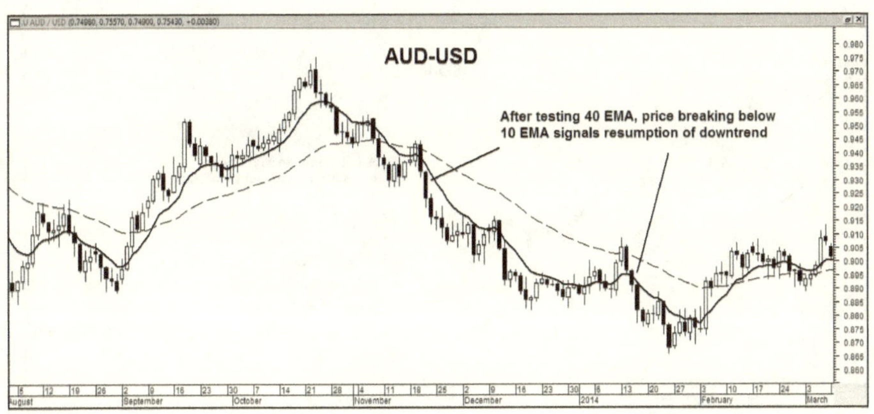

Chart 8.3(a) : Integrating 10/40 EMA downtrend with price weakness

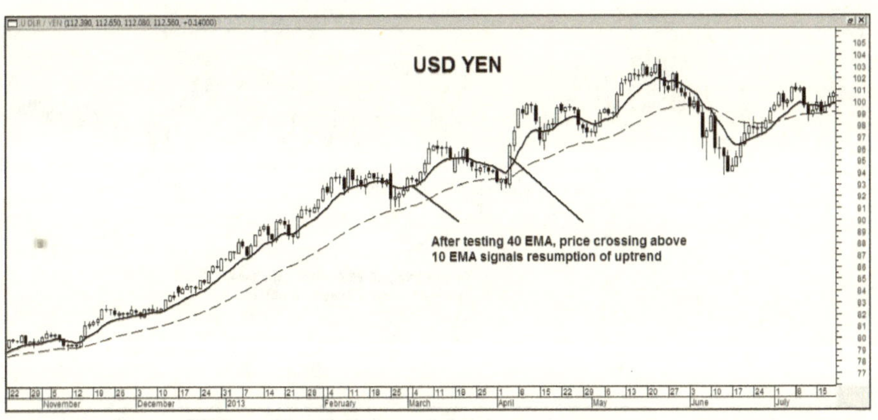

Chart 8.3(b) : Integrating 10/40 EMA uptrend with strong price action

(b) At the 40 EMA, candlesticks that suggest weakness such as black candlesticks with upper shadows provide signal the resumption of the down trend.

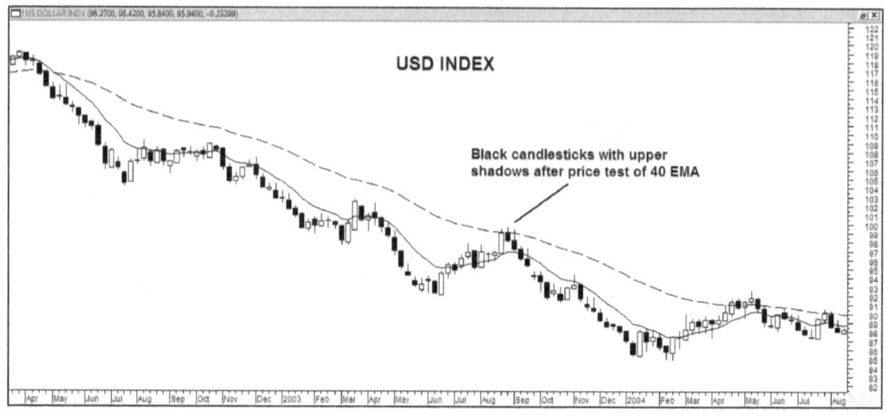

Chart 8.4(a) : Integrating 10/40 EMA downtrend with bearish candlesticks

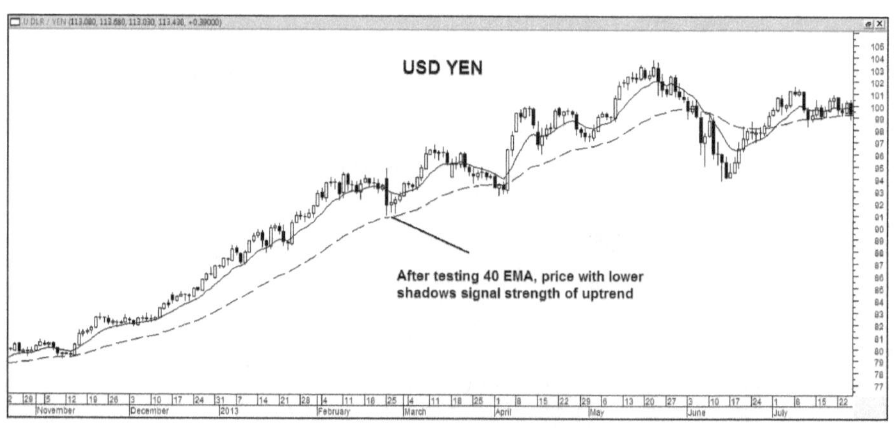

Chart 8.4(b) : Integrating 10/40 EMA uptrend with bullish candlesticks

(c) As price falls from 40 EMA or below 10 EMA, <u>breakaway gaps</u> and accompanying <u>long bars</u> (Chapter 2) to support the signal for the resumption of the downtrend.

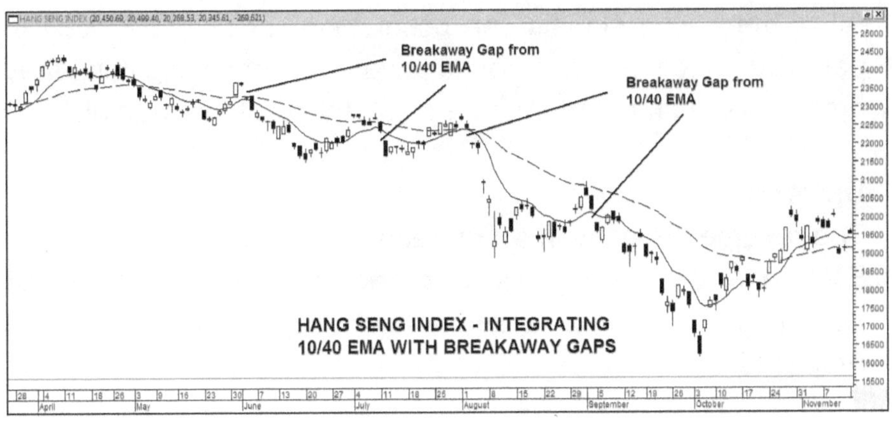

Chart 8.5: Integrating 10/40 EMA downtrend with Breakaway Gaps

(d) In a retracement up to 40 EMA, Stochastics typically rises above 50, possibly to 80. As price resumes down, <u>Stochastics %K crosses below %D</u>, triggering a sell signal and suggesting weakness.

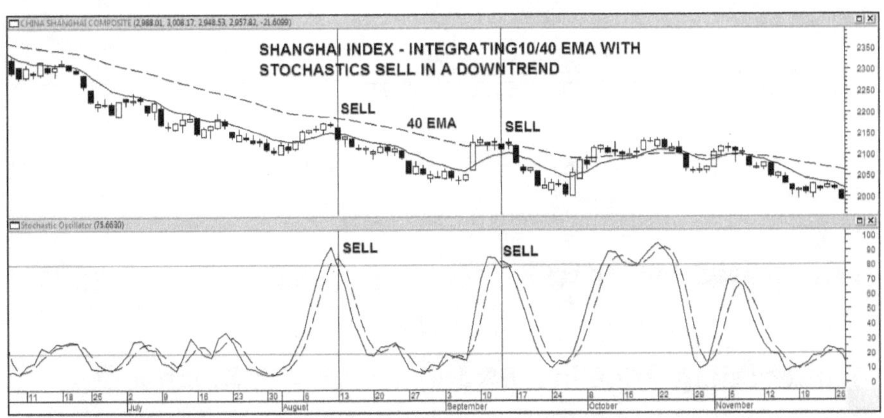

Chart 8.6: Integrating 10/40 EMA Downtrend with Stochastics Sell Entry signals

All of the above signals can occur together or more likely in part. But once an investor is aware of these signals, they greatly help him to formulate a correct view of the market.

Uptrend

The reverse happens in an uptrend. Price retraces down to 40 EMA and all the signals involving the resumption of the uptrend apply - price action, candlesticks, 10/40 EMA and Stochastics.

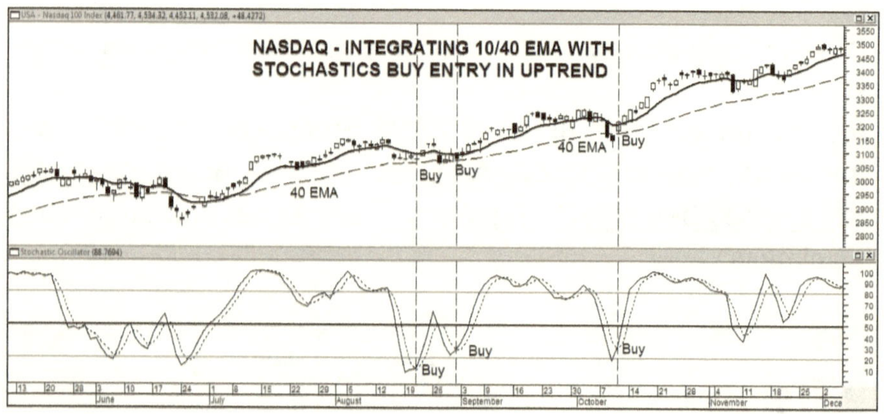

Chart 8.7: Integrating 10/40 EMA uptrend with Stochastics Buy Entry signals

TRENDING MARKETS

4. Integrating Price in a Strong Trend with Stochastics

In a strong trending market, whether up or down, <u>price does not break the 10 EMA</u>. Retracements are minimal and stop <u>at</u> the 10 EMA. This is not uncommon, and if one is waiting for a deeper retracement to buy at a better level, say the 40 EMA, one can wait "till the cows come home", and end up missing the entire trending move! This happens in a strong downtrend as well as uptrend.

This is a difficult technical situation because in the strong uptrend, when price is above the 10 EMA, Stochastics will be above 80 level (a sell level actually), but price simply continues up. Understandably, the investor does not feel safe to buy as Stochastics is above 80, yet the price continues to rise. If the price trades sideways but still above 10 EMA, Stochastics falls marginally below 80 level. At such high Stochastics level (60-70), one is naturally cautious about buying, but price may resume up again and Stochastics climbs above 80 again.

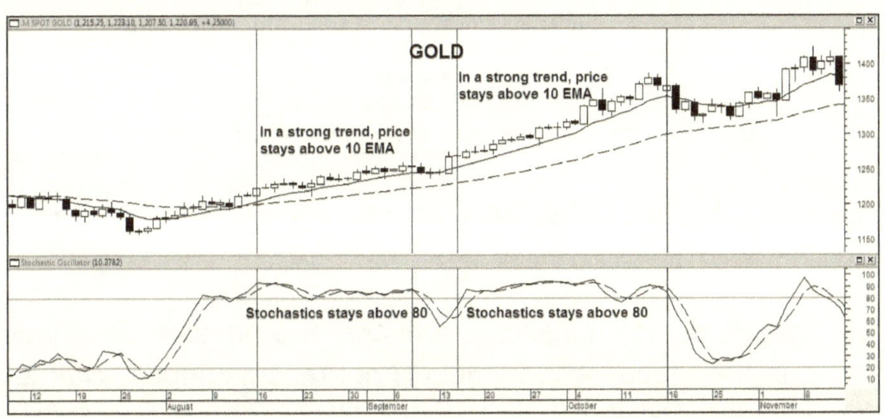

Chart 8.8: Integrating Price above 10 EMA with Stochastics in a Strong Uptrend

The same happens in the strong downtrend – price remains below the 10 EMA, and Stochastics remains below 20 (buy level), yet price continues to fall. If price moves sideways,

Stochastics may rise marginally above 20, but the investor is unlikely to sell at such a low Stochastics level.

This means that in a strong (up or down), the 10 EMA serves as the buy level or the sell level. Stochastics timing signals may have to be ignored under those circumstances. However, this is not a frequent situation, and it is best to treat this as an exception.

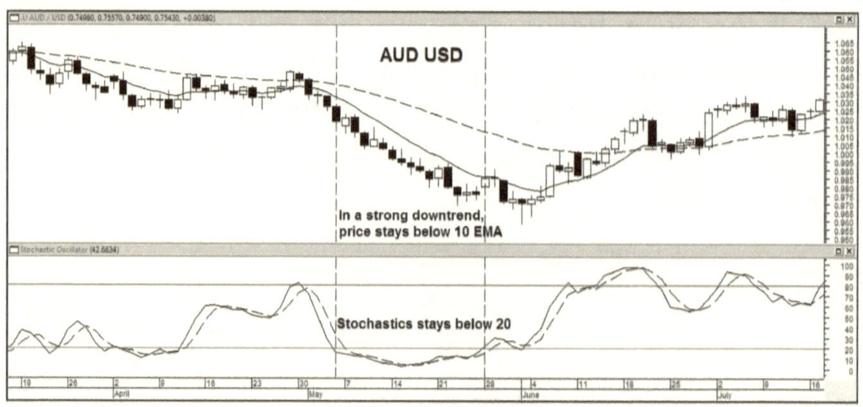

Chart 8.9: Integrating Price below 10 EMA with Stochastics in a Strong Downtrend

In the above circumstances, reducing the number of periods used in the Stochastics formula is not recommended, in order to maintain consistency and predictability.

CONGESTION

5. Integrating Candlesticks with Bollinger Bands & Stochastic in a Congest- ion

We found in Chapter 4 that Bollinger Bands is the unique indicator that provides support and resistance levels to investors in a congestion. Resistance is at the Upper Band, while support is at the Lower Band.

We also know that in a congestion, the Stochastics buy/sell signals are as follows:

Buy signal: Stochastics below 20 and %K crosses above %D.

Sell signal: Stochastics above 80 and %K crosses below %D.

(a) When price trades around the Upper Band, and %K is above 80, wait for it to cross below %D to trigger sell <u>in the region of the Upper Band</u>. Also when price trades around the Lower Band, and %K is below 20, wait for the cross-up signal to trigger a buy <u>in the region of the Lower Band</u>.

(b) It should be noted that there is no certainty that price will trade <u>at</u> the Upper or Lower Bands. Hence, should price fail to reach either Bands, and instead price turns near either band, and Stochastics %K does cross %D, then the Stochastics buy/sell signals are valid. On the other hand, price may trade out of either bands briefly or partially, which enables a buy or sell at the Upper/Lower Band.

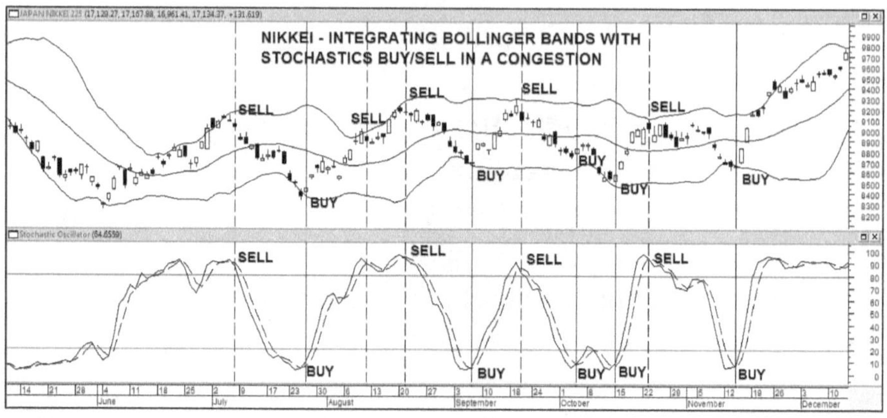

Chart 8.10: Integrating Bollinger Bands with Stochastics Buy/Sell signals in a Congestion

(c) Investors should note that when price trades to either Upper or Lower Bands, do watch for bearish candlesticks at the Upper Band, and bullish candlesticks at the Lower Band, which support a turn in the market.

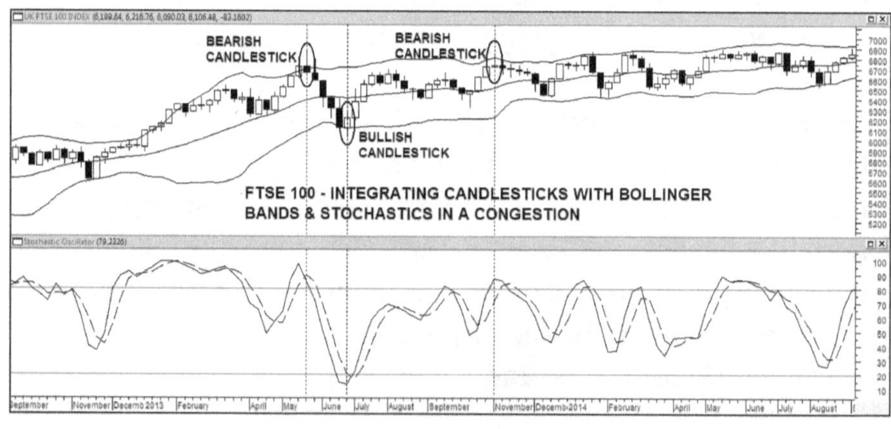

Chart 8.11: Integrating Bollinger Bands with Candlesticks & Stochastics in a Congestion

Conclusion

Integrating technical analysis is an important step in using technical analysis. The logic in integrating is in combining good signals from two or more reliable indicators to arrive at a better decision. I have found over the years that integration has worked in the market scenarios that are discussed in this chapter. However, the integration techniques here are certainly not the only ones that will work. Seasoned technical analysts will have more techniques in integrating indicators, and investors keen to develop other integration techniques should pursue more techniques for the future.

CHAPTER 9 - TIME FRAME TECHNIQUE FOR LONG-TERM INVESTMENT

Technical analysis is for long-term investments too - a breakthrough!

Technical analysis has long been associated with short-term trading. I believe that is because no definitive approach has been used to apply technical analysis for longer term investment, thus leaving the impression that it is only good for the short-term.

I have spent many years in pursuit of a method in technical analysis that works on a range of time frames, from shorter to longer term. This chapter explains my solution to that problem. It will show investors that it is vital to look at markets in more than one time frame in order to get a longer term view as is needed for investing rather than trading. The chapter will explain how to systematically link the different time frames so that it is possible at any one point in time to understand where markets are headed in the context of more than one time frame. This chapter will further explain how the important signals of the larger time frames can impact the movements of the shorter time frames, and vice versa. In all, this chapter will teach investors how to harness technical analysis for investment, and learn that it is not just for trading.

Defining Time Frame Technique

It is common practice for traders to look at markets in a <u>single</u> time frame, typically only the time frame they trade in, be it the hourly or daily charts. Charts are however, available on a whole range of time frames - from 5 minutes to hourly, daily, weekly, monthly, and beyond.

The Time Frame approach is the technique of analysing a market over two or more time frames. The 5-minute chart trader should analyse the hourly chart, while the Daily chart trader should analyse the Weekly chart or even the Monthly chart. A trader who is able to do that well will forecast a market better, and trade more effectively. An investor who wishes to use technical analysis for investing has to look beyond the daily chart to the weekly and monthly charts to arrive at longer term views of markets and make investment decisions based on the signals from the longer term charts.

Benefits of Time Frame Technique

Firstly, the time frame approach makes it possible to develop a whole range of views of a market, from the very short-term to the very long-term. An hourly chart provides a view of a market for a few days; a daily chart provides an outlook several weeks into the future; while a weekly chart provides the outlook several months ahead. A common myth that technical analysis is only good for short-term trades only reflects the fact that traders and investors are not aware of the fact that weekly and monthly charts provide a longer-term perspective of markets.

The second advantage of using the Time Frame technique is that the investor gets better perspective. An investor who buys on the strength of a Daily <u>uptrend</u> should be aware of the downside risks if the Weekly trend is <u>down</u>. The Weekly trend may eventually make itself felt despite the uptrend in the daily time frame. In the event that both daily and weekly time frames have the same trend, then the market is doubly strong.

Thirdly, the Time Frame approach removes the confusion surrounding the terms "short", "medium" and "long-term" trends. What is "short term" for one investor may be "long term" for another. When the time frame technique is used, an investor needs only to <u>define the trend by time frame used</u> – the hourly trend, the daily trend, weekly trend, the monthly trend, and so on. The challenge in the Time Frame approach is to integrate the trends of two or more time frames and resolve any conflicting signals between any two time frames.

Time Frame Principles

Principle 1: All valid technical signals in Daily charts are applicable in the larger time frames. This is true of <u>all</u> the indicators. So the trend signals, timing and price signals covered in this book are all valid in the larger time frames - 10/40 EMA, MACD, price patterns, candlestick patterns, Stochastics, Bollinger Bands, and Fibonacci.

This is an important Time Frame guideline because there is consistency in the indicators whichever time frame they are used. That is to say, a good indicator with powerful signals in a Daily chart works in a larger time frame as well. However, the impact of the signal in a larger time frame is greater, lasts longer, and perhaps is more important because of that.

Principle 2: The larger the time frame, the bigger the move, and vice versa.
A market's trend – uptrend, downtrend, congestion - is defined by the 10/40 EMA technique covered in Chapter 3. 10/40 EMA are to be used in the Weekly, Monthly and other time frames to signal the trend and the change in trend.

The magnitude of the weekly trend move is larger than that of a daily trend; while the magnitude of a monthly trend move is even larger than that of a weekly trend. One can conclude that once a weekly or monthly trend is in place, large moves will happen. This is something that investors need to get used to, especially for those who may follow markets on a day-to-day basis and therefore be used to smaller moves.

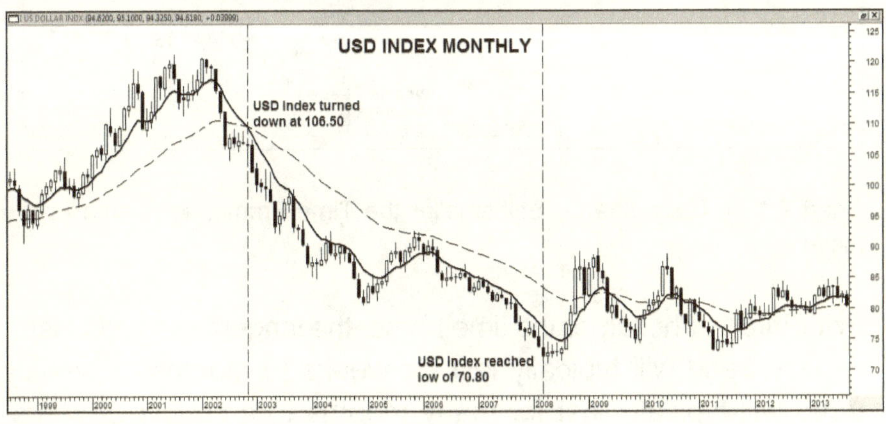

Chart 9.1(a): Monthly Chart - The bigger the Time Frame, the larger the move

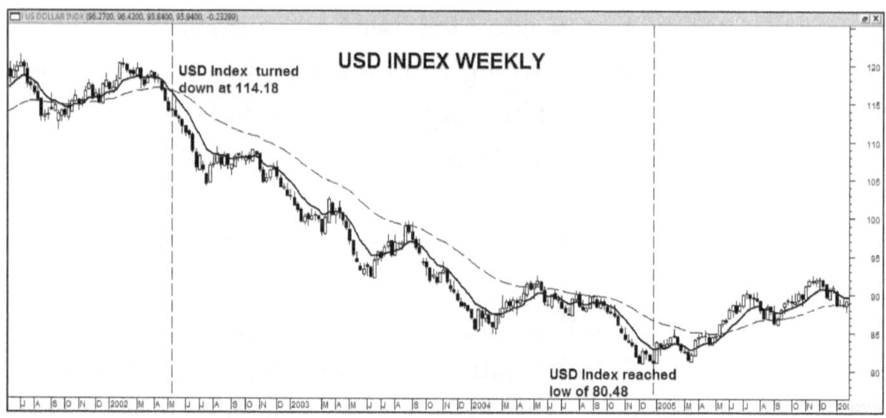

Chart 9.1(b): Weekly Chart - The smaller the Time Frame, the smaller the move

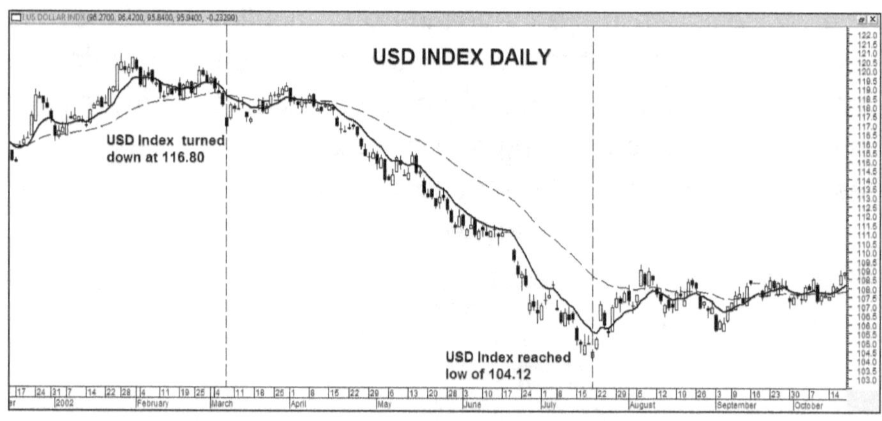

Chart 9.1(c): Daily Chart – Still smaller the Time Frame, even smaller the move

Principle 3: The larger the time frame, the longer the trends last. A daily trend will typically last for weeks to months. A weekly trend will typically last for many months to a couple of years, while a monthly trend will typically last several years.

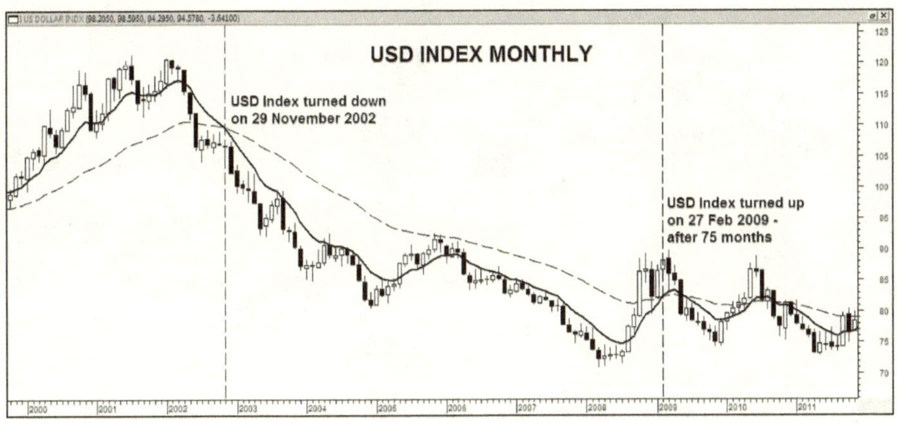

Chart 9.2(a): Monthly Chart - The bigger the Time Frame, the longer the trend lasts

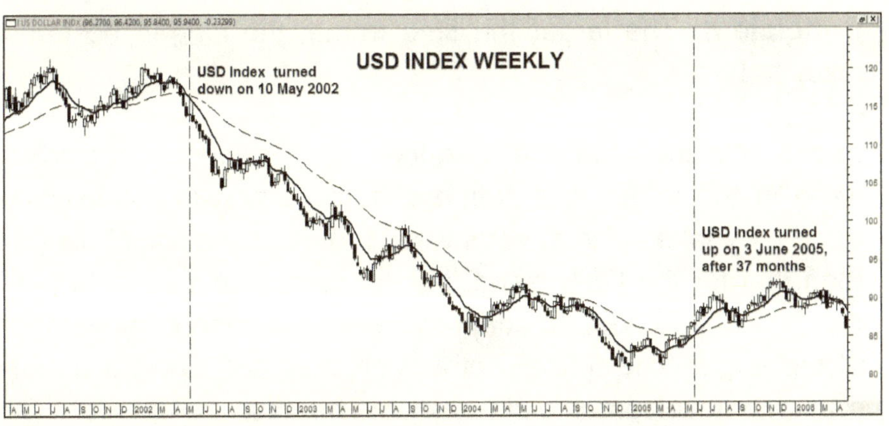

Chart 9.2(b): Weekly Chart - The smaller the Time Frame, the shorter the trend lasts

Chart 9.2(c) : Daily Chart - Still smaller the Time Frame, even the shorter the trend lasts

Principle 4: The larger the time frame, the longer the trend takes to turn

In line with the above, it therefore takes a longer time for a trend in the larger time frame to turn. A turn in the Weekly trend may take up to several weeks to complete, much longer than that for the Daily trend. Market participants used to only the daily charts need to adapt to the slower pace of movement of the larger time frames, otherwise they can end up out-of-step with developments in these time frames.

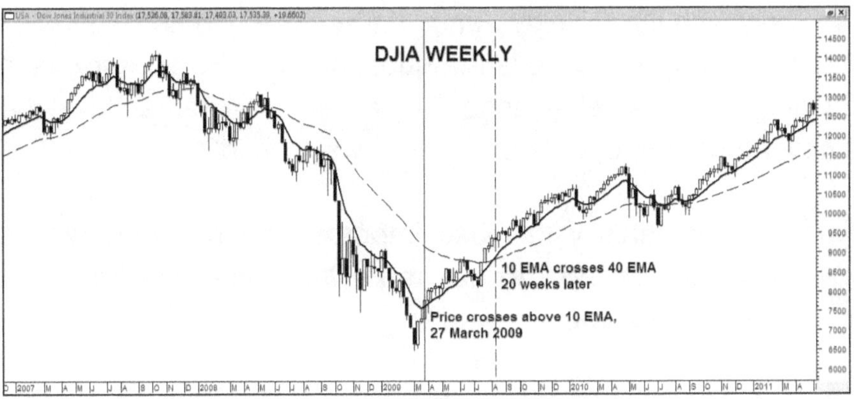

Chart 9.3(a) : <u>Weekly</u> Chart - the bigger the Time Frame, the longer the trend takes to turn

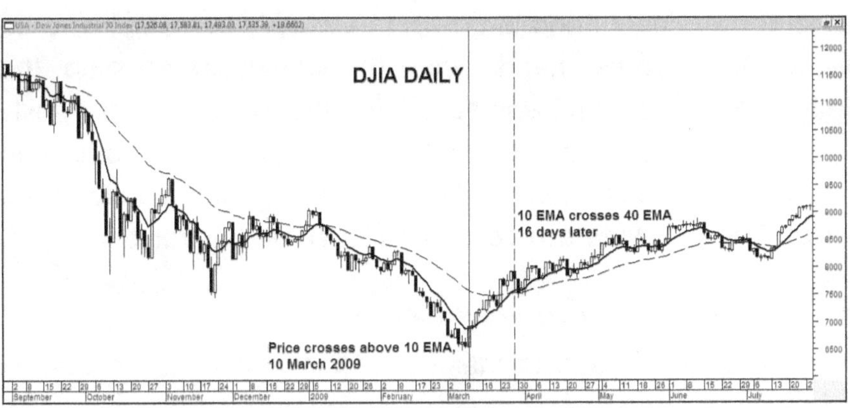

Chart 9.3(b) : Daily Chart - the smaller the Time Frame, the faster the trend takes to turn

4 Important Time Frame Relationships

In using the longer term charts for investment, it is not enough just to read the technical signals of one single time frame. This is because the investor will quickly encounter conflicting signals between the 2 or even 3 time frames. How to reconcile the Daily with the Weekly trends if there are opposing signals? Another important issue is the question of which time frame is "driving" the market – does the larger time frame drive the smaller time frame, or is it the other way round?

This section deals with these important relationships, which will throw light on how to use more than one time frame for investment purposes.

1st Time Frame Relationship: The larger trend drives the smaller trend.

When the weekly trend is down, the daily trend will be weak; when the monthly trend is down, the weekly trend will also be weak. On the other hand, when the weekly trend is up, the daily trend will be firm, and so on. In other words, if the weekly trend is down, one should not expect the daily trend to turn up easily as the weekly trend is likely to keep pushing daily prices down. The following two cases can illustrate this relationship.

Time Frame Case 1 COMEX GOLD
Using Monthly Charts to make a bearish forecast for Gold in Q2 of 2013

(a)   As at 28 February 2013, Gold Monthly bar fell and closed at 1,577.70, below the Monthly 10 EMA. While the Monthly 10 EMA was still above 40 EMA, Gold price falling below the Monthly 10 EMA (1,656.74) was a sign of weakness. Going by 10/40 EMA theory, the next objective was 40 EMA at 1,476.

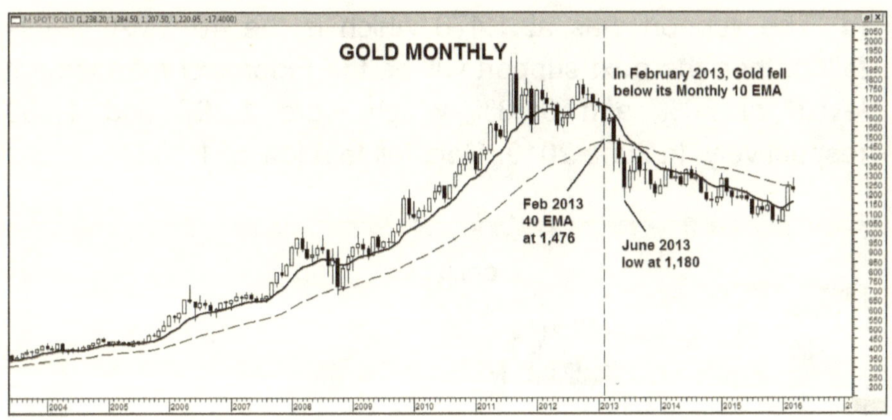

Chart 9.4(a) : COMEX Gold 2013 Q2 Outlook with Monthly 10/40 EMA

(b) Monthly Stochastics %K (at 41) and %D were both falling and still had potential to fall to the 20 level. Stochastics also suggested weakness in Gold!

(c) Monthly MACD line had crossed below Signal Line in February 2013 and was falling, another signal of weakness in Gold.

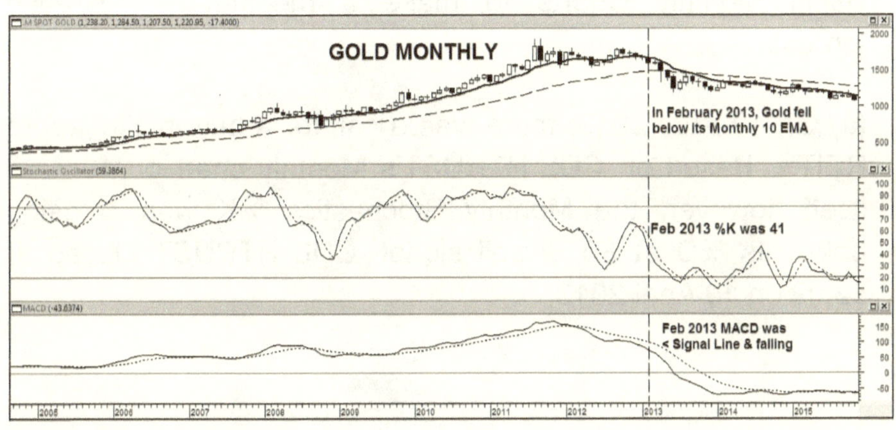

Chart 9.4(b) : COMEX Gold 2013 Q2 Outlook with Monthly 10/40 EMA, Stochastics & MACD

(d) The support was at 1,476 which is the 40 EMA. If this failed, then the next support will be the Fibonacci retracement levels of 50% and 61.8% which were 1,297 and 1,150 respectively. In June 2013, Gold fell to a low of 1,183.

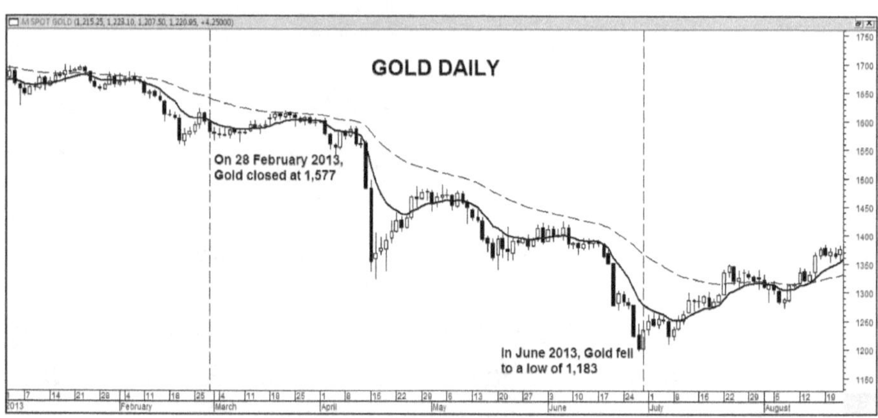

Chart 9.4(c) : COMEX Gold <u>Daily</u> was downtrend between February and June 2013

Time Frame Case 2 CDL HTRUST
Using Monthly Charts to make a medium-term bearish forecast

(a) On 19 April 2013, there was a call for a buy in Singapore REIT's. Based on CDL HTRUST's Monthly chart on 19 April itself however, the Monthly Stochastics %K was crossing below its %D at 80, a sell signal. CDL HTRUST closed at $2.09 on 19 April 2013.

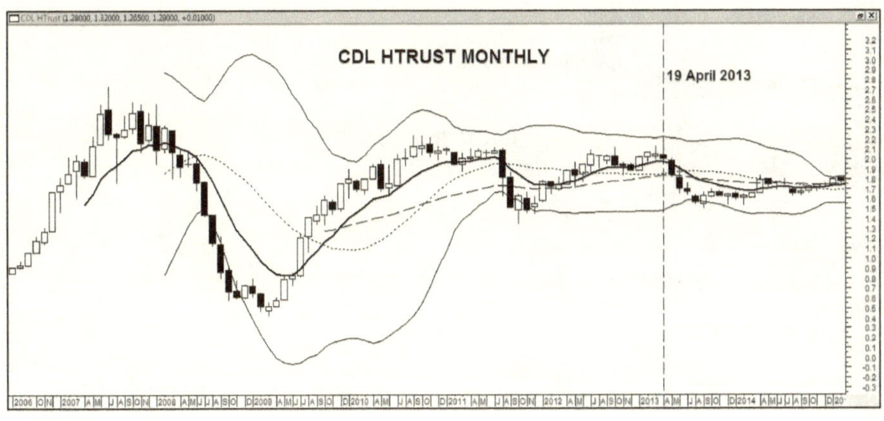

Chart 9.5(a) : CDL HTRUST Bearish Outlook with Monthly Chart

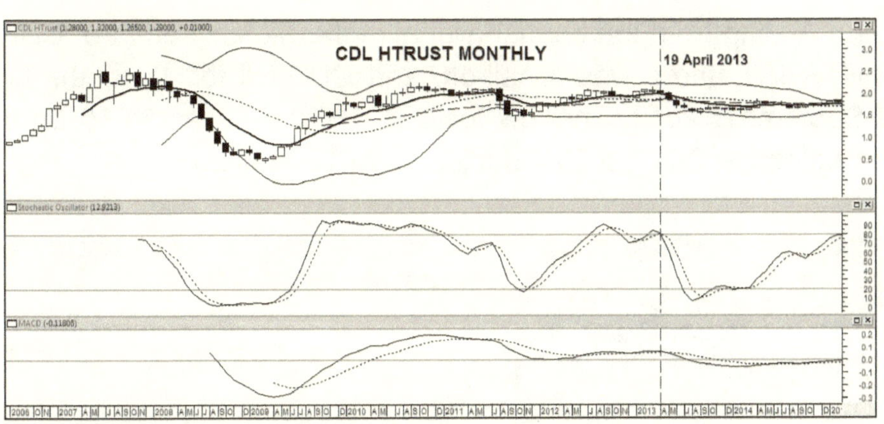

Chart 9.5(b) : CDL HTRUST Monthly Chart with sell signals from Stochastics & MACD

(b) However, based on the Daily Chart of CDL HTRUST on 19 April, there was no indication that any major move was imminent. CDL HTRUST was only congesting.

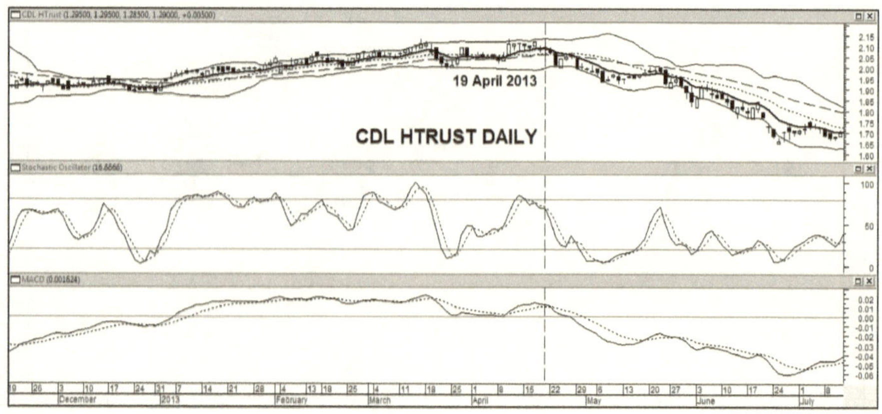

Chart 9.5(c) : CDL HTRUST <u>Daily</u> chart in a congestion as at 19 April 2013

(c) Arising from the bearish signal in the Monthly chart of CDL HTRUST, there was a sell-off, and CDL fell for 4 months till September 2013. The low for CDL HTRUST was $1.50 on 6 September 2013, a 28% decline from 19 April 2013.

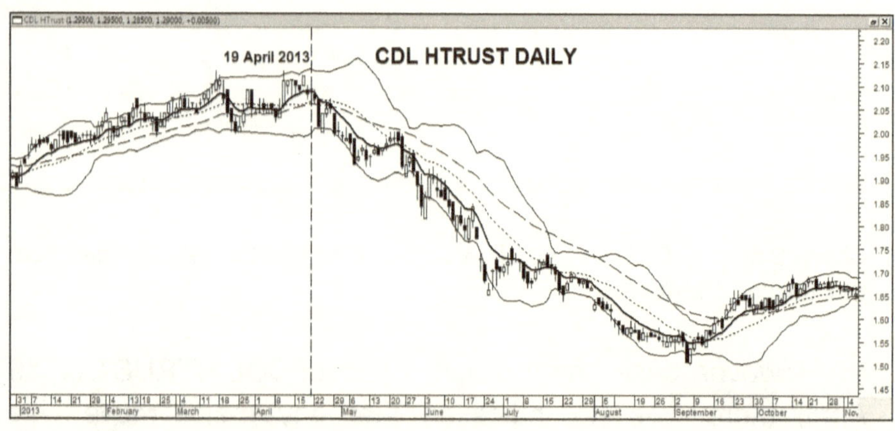

Chart 9.5(d) : CDL HTRUST <u>Daily</u> Chart in a major downtrend from 19 April to September 2013

2nd Time Frame Relationship: When the larger trend is up, the smaller trend can still be down. And vice versa.

If the Weekly trend is up, can the Daily trend turn down? It is possible - the Daily trend can turn down when the Weekly trend is undergoing a <u>retracement down</u>.

What is the objective of the Daily downtrend when the move is seen in the context of the Weekly retracement? From the 10/40 EMA technique, we know that typically the 40 EMA will be the limit of a normal retracement. So the Weekly 40 EMA can be used to project the limit of the daily downtrend when it is part a Weekly retracement. This development can be observed in markets.

Time Frame Case 3 DAX 30
When the Weekly Uptrend is retracing down, the DAX 30 Daily will be on a downtrend.

(a) In July 2012, DAX 30 Weekly turned uptrend, 10 EMA crossed above 40 EMA. In April and in June 2013, DAX 30 Weekly retraced down <u>below</u> its 10 EMA, but was supported at 40 EMA.

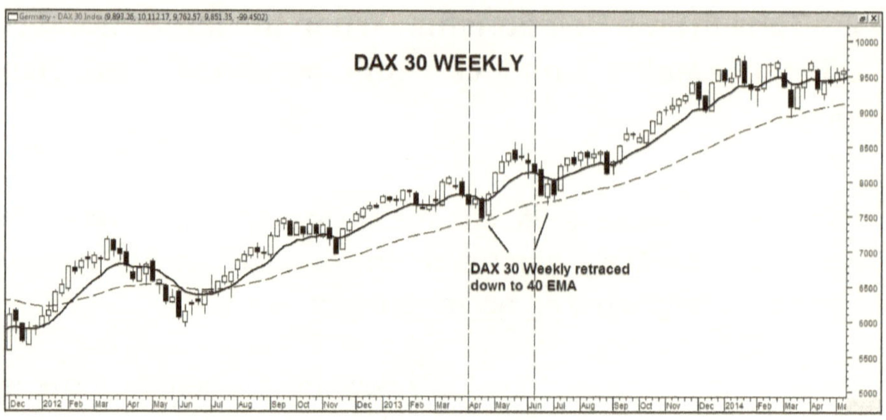

Chart 9.6(a) : DAX 30 <u>Weekly</u> Index retraced below 10 EMA in April & June 2013, but supported at 40 EMA

(b) At the same time that the Weekly chart corrected down in April and June, the DAX 30 Daily 10 EMA crossed below its 40 EMA. In other words, a downtrend occurred in the Daily chart. This shows that it is possible for the Daily trend to be down for a short period when the Weekly uptrend is having its retracement down.

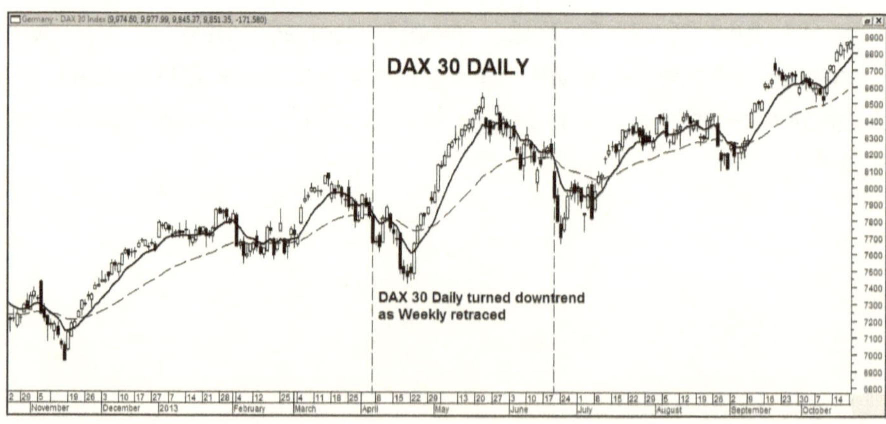

Chart 9.6(b): DAX 30 <u>Daily</u> turned downtrend as Weekly DAX 30 retraced down

(c) The same is true in a Weekly downtrend retracing up. The same is also true in a Monthly-Weekly relationship.

3rd Time Frame Relationship: If the larger trend drives the smaller trend, is it possible for the smaller trend to turn the larger trend?

It can. The smaller trend can overcome the larger trend if it makes a sustained and large move.

If there is a Weekly and Daily downtrend, the daily trend will have to first turn up, i.e. Daily 10 EMA crosses above 40 EMA for the Daily trend to turn the Weekly trend. After a Daily 10/40 EMA turn up, if price action continues to rise strongly and in a sustained manner, it will push price towards the Weekly 40 EMA, and subsequently the Weekly 10 EMA towards the Weekly 40 EMA. Eventually the Weekly 10 EMA will rise above the 40 EMA, resulting in the weekly trend to change as well.

Time Frame Case 4 USD-YEN
Daily trend turning the Weekly & Monthly trends

(a) Monthly USD-YEN was on a downtrend from December 2007. The Monthly bars remained <u>below</u> the Monthly 10 EMA all the way till January 2012.

Chart 9.7(a) : USD Yen Monthly Chart was down from 2007

(b) Daily USD-YEN turned uptrend on 1 November 2011, when Daily 10 EMA crossed above 40 EMA.

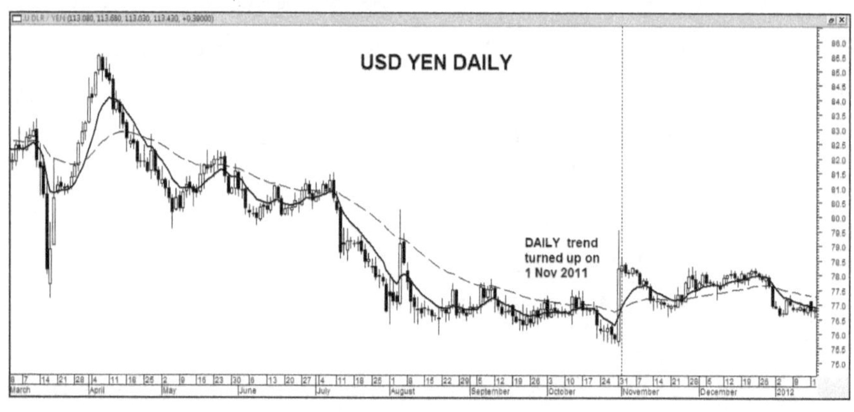

Chart 9.7(b) : USD-Yen Daily Chart turned uptrend on 1 November 2011

(c) On the back of a sustained Daily uptrend, the Weekly USD-YEN turned uptrend on 2 March 2012, a significant development.

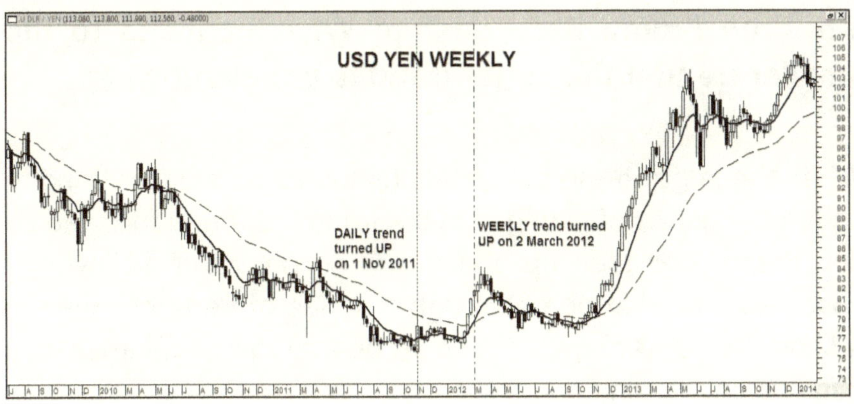

Chart 9.7(c) : USD-Yen Weekly Chart turned uptrend on 2 March 2012 as a result of sustained Daily uptrend

(d) Eventually, with the continued strength in the Daily and Weekly trends, USD-YEN broke <u>above</u> the Monthly 10 EMA in February 2012, and the Monthly 40 EMA in December 2012. USD-YEN's Monthly 10 EMA eventually crossed above its 40 EMA at the end of March 2013, turning the Monthly trend up.

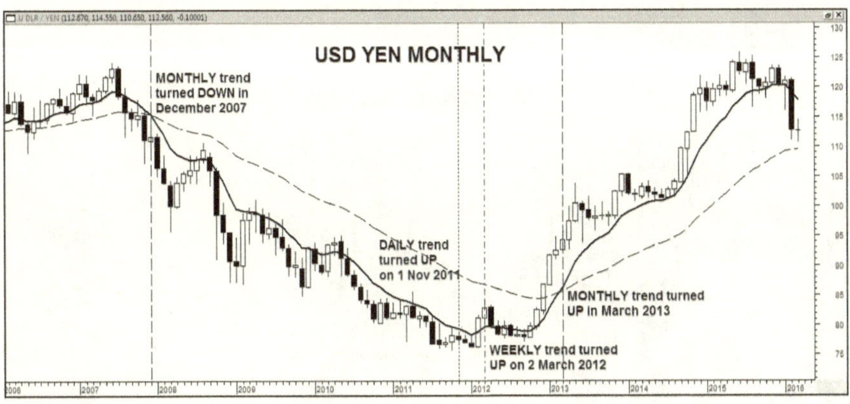

Chart 9.7(d) : USD Yen <u>Monthly</u> Chart turned uptrend by end-March 2013 as a result of Daily and Weekly trends' sustained uptrend

4th Time Frame Relationship: What happens to the smaller trend if the larger trend is congesting?

When the larger trend congests, it causes the smaller trend to undergo a series of changes in the trend – uptrend followed by downtrend, and then up again, and so on. So if an investor observes a market goes through a series of trend changes in a shorter time frame, then it could be that the next larger time frame is undergoing congestion.

Time Frame Case 5 LIGHT CRUDE
Weekly trend congestion causes daily trend to turn up and down

Weekly Light Crude was congesting in for the period September 2012 and May 2013, trading between 99.50 high and 84.00 low. The can be seen from the 10/40 EMA criss-crossing, and also price trading within the Bollinger Upper and Lower Bands.

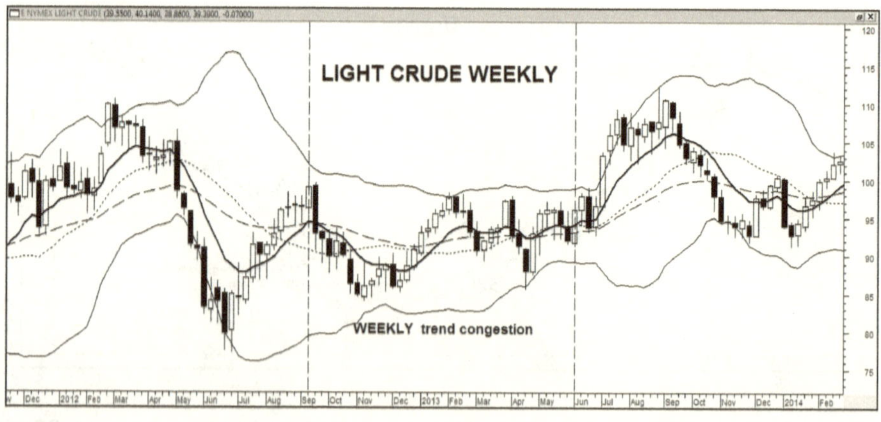

Chart 9.8(a) : Light Crude Weekly trend congestion

However, for the same period, the Daily trend was going through a series of uptrend and downtrend, as evidenced by the 10/40 EMA action.

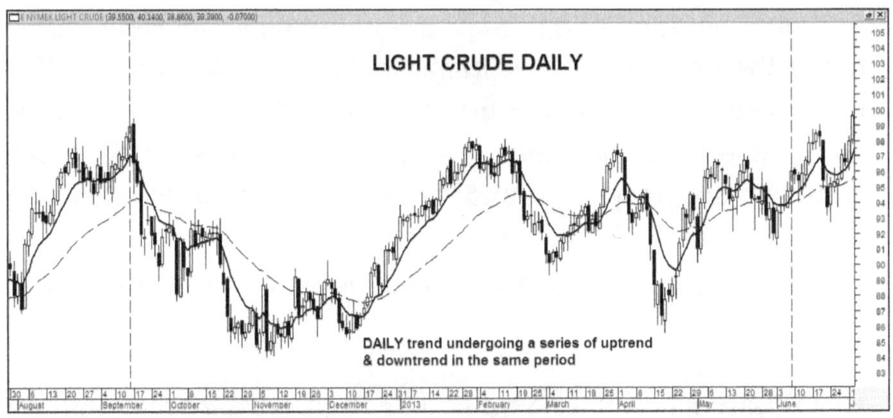

Chart 9.8(b) : Light Crude Weekly congestion caused <u>Daily</u> trend to turn up and down

Time Frame Guidelines

1. When using the Time Frame technique, adopt a top-down approach - start with the larger time frame first, and work down to the smaller time frame. <u>Not the other way round</u>. For example, look at a 10/40 EMA in the Monthly, then the Weekly and finally the Daily.

2. Use the same indicators for the same function – 10/40 EMA for trend, Stochastics and MACD for timing. Price patterns and candlestick patterns are valid in all time frames.

3. Use the same parameters for the technical indicators used to achieve consistency in the signals in the larger time frames.

Eg, 10/40 EMA for Weekly or Monthly charts, 13 periods for Stochastics, default MACD, 20 SMA plus 2 standard deviation for Bollinger Bands, etc for Weekly and Monthly charts.

4. When the trend of a particular time frame is not clear, zoom out to the next larger time frame to get a clearer picture. This is consistent with the first guideline stated above. If the next time frame is still not clear, then zoom out yet again. One can start with the Daily trend and move all the way to the Monthly. Zooming out will eventually provide a clearer view of a market's trend, and the relationship between the different time frames.

5. Analyse different time frame charts at regular time intervals - weekly charts to be reviewed at the end of each week; monthly charts at month-end, and so one. One should not analyse the larger charts until the period has ended.

6. It is important to note that the integration of indicators (Chapter 8) that works for the Daily time frame works too in the larger time frames. Hence investors should master the integration techniques as the impact of the techniques in larger time frames can only have greater impact and assume even more importance.

Making the Most of Time Frames

1. To make the most of the time frames technique, investors have to know indicators well because the signals are the same in the different time frames.

2. Using more indicators will provide more signals to strengthen the analysis. Eg, be prepared to use more than one trend indicator, and more indicators for support/ resistance levels. The reason for this is one indicator may not be adequate for different time frames. So it helps to use more.

3. The Weekly chart is the important time frame to keep track of the bigger trends. If the Daily trend appears to be overbought and nearing a top, but the Weekly trend is not, then the market may continue its move. The same can be said for the downtrend.

4. The Monthly chart and beyond takes a much longer time to produce signals, and monthly charts become relevant only when large moves are taking place, eg the stock market decline in 2008/09, or the Gold price decline in 2012 and 2013. This however does not mean that investors should not follow the Monthly charts - they should, but they should appreciate that the Monthly trend will take longer to take its effect.

5. Triple Time Frame
If the market is making a big move, and even the Weekly chart is not able to read the market, then it becomes necessary to use the Monthly chart as well. Analysis then becomes more complex, involving 3 time frames. The focus will then shift to the Monthly and Weekly charts. However the underlying relationship between the Monthly and the Weekly trends is still governed by the 4 primary relationships discussed in the earlier section. The Daily time frame then becomes less

important, and the Weekly and Monthly time frames become more important.

Conclusion

Time Frames is a complex topic; just understanding the gyrations of a market in a single time frame is complicating enough. So to attempt to understand more than one time frame plus linking two or more of them is even more challenging. But I hope this chapter will help investors who want to use technical analysis for investments to start on this journey. For me the journey has taken close to 20 years and it is still not completed. But to me it is a journey that is well worth embarking on!

CHAPTER 10 - MANAGING POSITIONS

Investments have to be managed – Ignore at your own risk!

While learning technical analysis adds a whole new dimension to investing better, I have observed over the years that investors make serious mistakes in managing positions. This aspect of managing investments is independent of technical analysis and is worth while paying more attention to. Beyond basic principles such as trading with the trend, cutting your losses short and letting your profits run, investors can do more to manage their positions better to attain better outcome.

Fear and Greed

We often hear about the psychology of fear and greed in investment. After a market has been made a sizeable move up, investors tend to be lulled into thinking the trend is still strong. This is the "greed" factor, and investors will still buy at high levels in the belief that the market will get even higher. At the same time, analysts may be forecasting even higher levels, stoking investor sentiments further. The investor ends up <u>buying high,</u> even at record highs! When the market eventually turns, they wonder why they bought so high!

On the other hand, it is only after a market has fallen considerably that "fear" sets in causing investors to panic, to cut out their buys and end up <u>selling low</u>. They live with "hope" that the market's move against them will end soon. Investors thus end up making a major loss instead of making minor losses by cutting their positions earlier. Investors are thus caught in this web of greed and fear.

Investors must not allow these two powerful forces of greed and fear get the better of them. Of course this is certainly one of the hardest things to do, and it takes a lot of discipline, but it is well worth the effort.

But how does the investor know that a market has made a sizeable move and he should not be buying high or selling low? The answer lies in the Time Frame technique, watching monthly and weekly signals instead of following only Daily charts as discussed in Chapter 9.

Pyramiding

What if an investor still wishes to buy into a market that has risen sizeably? After all we don't really know where is the market's final top. The solution is to refrain from aggressive trades. If you have to enter new positions at weekly or monthly chart highs, it makes sense to enter smaller positions. The higher the market, the smaller the absolute position size. This is the principle of Pyramiding.

Pyramiding makes a lot of sense because if smaller positions are opened at higher levels, a sudden turn in the market will affect the investor less than if the positions are larger.

Lower Price Stocks

Stock investors can better manage positions when the market is high by buying lower priced stocks rather than higher price ones in case a sudden reversal occurs. A 10% drop in a $0.50 stock is the same as a 10% drop in a $5.00 stock in relative terms. But a 10% drop in a $5.00 stock is very different in absolute terms compared to a 10% drop in the $0.50 stock. It makes a very different impact on the absolute capital risked.

Partial Exit

After markets have made a major move, investors should consider exiting part of their positions. For example, sell 5 lots out of a holding of 10 lots.

Alternatively, investors can exit profitable stock positions that are moving less aggressively. Do not try and get the last cent out of a move especially if the monthly or weekly charts are showing signs of slowing down.

The "Crowded Trade"

Avoid the herd mentality. In early 2013, gold was probably the most popular investment. But by the second quarter of 2013, gold price fell sharply, suffering its biggest fall in three decades. Many investors would have bought the metal because it was the most 'obvious' and popular trade. It is human to do what everyone else is doing, but in investing, contrary opinions can be safer.

Managing Long Term Positions

Investors must not forget their positions just because they are "long term" ones. This is one of the more common and serious errors in investing – investors do not exit their positions. In my experience, investors are more focused about getting into the market, but not when it comes to getting out.

Investors are all busy with work, family and social lives. So when a position is profitable, they just let it run and take no action. But markets move in trends, and eventually they do turn and that can wipe out what was previously a good position. Therefore it makes sense for investors to monitor their investments, if not daily at least weekly. Choosing a good time to exit may not be simple, but leaving it alone is certainly not an option.

On Following Recommendations

Do not follow recommendations blindly. Investors need to do their own homework to assess investment recommendations, even from "reputable opinions". It makes a lot of sense not to follow recommendations blindly no matter how well intentioned they are. In April 2013, a financial institution put forward a buy recommendation for a popular investment instrument. Upon referring to my Weekly and Monthly charts, I found that all the recommended stocks had already made major moves up to April. The downside risk was obvious to me. Soon after, the sector declined up to 25%!   Investors must have a good method of analysing investment recommendations, whether it is fundamental or technical analysis. But it should be done, after all it is his own capital that is being risked.

Your Own Portfolio of Preferred Stocks

Investors should regularly review their portfolio – is it messy, are you happy with it? Are there too many stocks, the result of following too many recommendations in the past? Are there too many positions opened on impulse? The result is that an inordinate amount of the investor's capital is tied up, leaving insufficient funds for the really good investment idea that comes along.

Investors should review their portfolio regularly, say every 6 months, and re-align it so that they can be ready for the good positions. All investors big or small have limited resources, so it makes sense to plan ahead and set aside money for future investments.

An Investment Model that Suits You

Investors can adopt either a short-term trading or a long-term investment perspective that suits their temperament or style. A short-term trading style of getting in and out of markets over a few days means more work, and more stress. If you are a retiree or a homemaker, you may have more time to focus on shorter term trades. But if you have a busy lifestyle that combines a hectic career, then a short-term trading model will be harder to sustain.

Also, investors who adopt short-term 'trading' model should not forget that at times markets do get into big and sustained moves. But by then, the trader may have exited the market and fails to take advantage of the big move.

Conclusion

This chapter suggests some ideas for investors to manage their positions better; some of these ideas are built upon the technical analysis that is covered in the early chapters of this book. However some of the other suggestions are just common sense ideas that are often overlooked or ignored at great expense to investors.

CONCLUDING REMARKS

Of the techniques covered in this book, a number of them are original and they have taken some years to be formulated and tested by the author. Even for seasoned users of technical analysis, the chapters on Integration and Time Frame may still be new and need some effort. But for investors new to technical analysis, it is recommended that you take your time through the book to "test" and observe the effectiveness of the many techniques before "trusting" them. However I believe all readers will find it worth it to invest their time and effort into the techniques.

Although this book has been written for the investor and to focus on longer term investment, traders with shorter term perspective can still benefit from the book. Integration of trend, timing and price is applicable in the daily time frame. For traders, the main difference is that they may not look beyond the weekly time frame. Beyond the weekly charts, signals are much slower and therefore not relevant. For investors, monthly or even quarterly charts maybe very relevant.

In the practical matter of software and price data, I would suggest that investors new to technical analysis invest in a good basic software so that they can better apply the techniques in this book in their markets. It is also recommended that the software be accompanied by a price data package with adequate price history to enable the time frame technique be applied effectively. For weekly charts, a minimum of 5 years of historical price data is needed; for monthly charts, a minimum of 15 years of price data is recommended. Having both a software and price data package will also give the investor the opportunity to explore learn new technical tools for the long run.

I wish all who have invested in this book the very best in their investment journey.

BC LOW – Chartist, Trader, Educator, Author

Boon-Chin Low has been a teacher-cum-practitioner in technical analysis since 1990. He created two original approaches in technical analysis which have been featured in the US magazine, "Technical Analysis of Stocks & Commodities" in 2010 and 2012. BC was awarded the Chartered Market Technician (CMT) by Market Technicians Association in 2000. He was Senior Lecturer in Singapore Polytechnic, and pioneered the teaching of technical analysis in the polytechnic from 1991 to 2011. He is currently President of Technical Analysis Consultancy (www.taconsultancy.biz). He was President of the Singapore Technical Analysts & Traders Society (STATS) in 2011-13. BC was previously Technical Analyst at Merrill Lynch International Bank in Singapore.

Other Publications By The Author

1. "Chart Your Future", PRESTIGE (SINGAPORE) November 2013

2. "Identifying a Trend with Directional Movement Index", TECHNICAL ANALYSIS OF STOCKS & COMMODITIES (United States), November 2012

3. "Trading, Time Frames & Trends", TECHNICAL ANALYSIS OF STOCKS & COMMODITIES (United States), September 2010

4. "Serious Trader's Perspective", BUSINESS TIMES (SINGAPORE) 1 September 2008,

5. Futures & Options Study Guide Chapter on Technical Analysis, Institute of Banking & Finance (IBF) Singapore, 1997.